BELGIUM AND THE FEBRUARY REVOLUTION

BRISON D. GOOCH

BELGIUM AND THE FEBRUARY REVOLUTION

THE HAGUE
MARTINUS NIJHOFF
1963

PRINTED IN THE NETHERLANDS

PREFACE

Adding to the growing body of literature on 1848, this study amplifies the political and diplomatic posture of Belgium both before and after the February Revolution. The narrative is based on diplomatic and administrative correspondence, most of it unpublished, and also on the papers of Charles Rogier and Sylvain Van de Weyer, now part of the holdings of Belgium's Archives Générales du Royaume. These materials make possible a more complete account of the Liberal Ministry's first year in office, a fuller treatment of the impact of the February Revolution on the Belgian domestic scene, and, for the first time, a detailed tracing of Belgian negotiations with the new Provisional Government and other European powers during the few months just after the fall of Louis Philippe. To my knowledge this is also the first monographic work in English to discuss Belgian problems in 1847 and 1848.

* * * *

I should like here to record my indebtedness. My greatest obligation is to the Belgian American Educational Foundation whose support was not only contributory to this study but also led to a major step in my personal intellectual growth. Transportation to Belgium was once provided by the Massachusetts Institute of Technology and typing of the manuscript was the work of Miss Carolyn Embach of the University of Oklahoma Faculty Research Committee. Among many archivists and librarians who have readily assisted my efforts, particular mention must be made of P.-H. Desneux, Chef du Service des Archives, and Mme. Nisol, both at Belgium's Archives du Ministère des Affaires Etrangères et du Commerce Extérieure.

BRISON D. GOOCH

TABLE OF CONTENTS

ABBREVIATIONS*

AEB   Belgium. Archives du Ministère des Affaires Etrangères et du Commerce Extérieure. Reference is to series of *Correspondance Politique* unless otherwise indicated.

AEF   France. Archives du Ministère des Affaires Etrangères. Reference is to *Correspondance Politique: Légations* series unless otherwise indicated.

AEV   Archives des affaires étrangères, Vienne. Series at AEB (10.945). Copies of correspondence to and from Austrian ambassador in Brussels.

CNB   A. de Ridder, ed., *La crise de la neutralité belge de 1848: le dossier diplomatique* (2 vols., Bruxelles, 1928). An important sampling of AEB holdings in the *Correspondance Politique* series for 1848.

DD   Charles H. Pouthas, ed., *Documents diplomatiques du Gouvernement provisoire et de la Commission du pouvoir exécutif* (2 vols., Paris, 1953–54). Sampling of AEF holdings in the *Correspondance Politique* series for 1848.

DM   *Départements Ministériels et Autorités Belges.* Series at AEB. Vol. 5 contains 347 entries covering 1847–1850.

F.O.   Great Britain. Foreign Office correspondence at the Public Record Office.

HP   Louis Hymans, *Histoire Parlementaire de la Belgique de 1831 à 1880* (5 vols., Bruxelles, 1878–1880).

IND   *Indépendance, neutralité, et défense militaire de la Belgique.* Series at AEB.

LV   Arthur C. Benson and Viscount Esher, eds., *The Letters of Queen Victoria* (3 vols., London, 1907). Vol. 2 covers 1844–1853.

RP   Charles Rogier Papers at the Archives Générales du Royaume in Belgium. Folio numbers cited are the old numbers as given in

* Many of the cited letters are drafts and virtually all were confidential.

the "Table de Concordance" in R. Boumans, *Inventaire des papiers de Charles Rogier* (Bruxelles, 1958), pp. 54–55. All letters cited "Rogier" refer to Charles unless otherwise indicated. Some of Rogier's letters are still held privately by Commandant G. Cuissart de Grelle who assured me (letter of Nov. 6, 1959) that none of these concern Rogier's public career.

VWP Sylvain Van de Weyer Papers at the Archives Générales du Royaume in Belgium. For data on these papers, see Lucienne van Meerbeeck, *Inventaire des Papiers de Sylvain Van de Weyer* (Bruxelles, 1960).

CHAPTER I

THE LIBERALS TAKE OFFICE

Introduction

As the nineteenth century approached its mid-point, European social stability as maintained by Metternich was entering a period of crisis. Smatterings of liberal aspirations coupled with unemployment created festering sources of potential trouble. This bridled unrest and uneasiness finally burst forth in the torrent of riots and revolutions still associated with 1848. The situation in Europe during and just after 1848 was fluid and volcanic as "The Revolution" had tentatively destroyed the grounds for certainty and both governments and men lived from day to day.

After February of 1848, while the impetus for Europe's woes seemed to come from France, in nearby Belgium a new government weathered the enveloping maelstrom. The young state managed to escape the full force of contagious revolution then running at flood tide over most of Europe but the margin of safety was narrow. This small nation suffered from a number of divisive influences which were encouraged by the February Revolution in France. The frustration of these forces (that is, Belgium's near-revolution) forms the milieu in which the Belgian government conducted its foreign affairs from mid-1847 through mid-1848.[1] This period of Belgian diplomacy, in its context of acute domestic issues, is the subject of this study.[2]

* * *

[1] See Woyna to Metternich, May 15, 1847, AEV, for acute analysis of Belgian social weaknesses and problems. Of particular interest is Woyna's estimate that the state of crisis in Belgium would be of no general importance if peace continued in Europe.

[2] This short but important period is sketched briefly in Henri Pirenne, *Histoire de Belgique* (7 vols., Bruxelles, 1900–32), VII, 130–148. For a more detailed narrative, see Ernest Discailles, *Charles Rogier (1800–1885), d'après des documents inédits* (4 vols., Bruxelles, 1893–95), II, 133–207. Though Discailles' work is regarded as "only a long dithyramb in four volumes" by Carlo Bronne, *Jules Van Praet* (Bruxelles, 1943), p. 42, it is nonetheless the best work on Charles Rogier. For fine bibliographies on various aspects of the reign of Leopold I (1535 entries), see A. Cosemans and Th. Heyse, *Contribution à la bibliographie dynastique et nationale: Bijdrage tot de bibliografie van vorstenhuis en land*, II, in *Cahiers belges et congolaises* (Bruxelles, 1944–), Nos. 24–25.

Belgium's government in 1848 was in the hands of its Liberal Party. Led by Charles Rogier, the Liberals had won an undisputed victory at the polls in 1847. Rogier was one of the "heroes of 1830" and with his colleagues had cooperated with the Catholic Party in bringing the new country and king through the decade of the thirties. When the question of national survival seemed settled after 1839, the semblance of political truce disappeared and gradually the Liberal Party gained ascendancy.[1]

Prior to the election in 1847 word leaked that King Leopold found his crown boring and that he was considering an extended trip to Italy and Sicily. In this case he would leave the queen as regent, an action reported to Metternich as the equivalent of giving the reins of the monarchy over to the King of the French, father of the queen. This plan was cancelled for a briefer trip into Germany. Shortly after the election and the cabinet had resigned, Leopold traveled to London and to Paris, prolonging the period of interim government. These absences at crucial periods upset and annoyed Rogier and other politicians as well.[2] Only with reluctance and amidst rumors of abdication [3] had Leopold finally turned to Rogier for the formation of a ministry.

As the Dutch menace had receded into the past, Leopold began to state his opinions freely and with a minimum of tact. Writing sarcastically about Rogier, he called the constitution "absurd" and maintained that really the monarchy had been "the rock on which the country's political life had exclusively rested." [4] After a Liberal cabinet became a certainty, Leopold explained condescendingly to Rogier that Belgium was "poor in political ideas" and "often disposed to lose sight of its real basis as an European state." His view was that there were two types of states, those created by force and those created by circumstances. Belgium was one of the latter and, Leopold ponti-

[1] For Liberal-Catholic participation in power prior to 1847, see Colette Lebas, *L'Union des Catholiques et des Libéraux de 1839 à 1847: Etude sur les pouvoirs exécutif et législatif* (Louvain, 1960).

[2] Woyna to Metternich, May 11, 1847, AEV; and Rumigny to Guizot, July 13, 1847, AEF, Belg., XXIX, where Rumigny presents an extensive analysis of the current Belgian political situation. See also Paul Hymans, *Frère-Orban* (2 vols., Bruxelles, [1905]), I, 163.

[3] Rumigny to Guizot, July 31, 1847, AEF, Belg., XXIX. These rumors, of uncertain origin, circulated both in the cities and countryside. Leopold later referred to how he had been "desirous of retiring from politics." See Leopold to Victoria, Mar. 25, 1848, LV, II, 196–197; and Discailles, *Rogier*, III, 163–168.

[4] Leopold to Nothomb, Jan. 16, 1846, and to Metternich, April 21, 1846, in Carlo Bronne, ed., *Lettres de Leopold Ier* (Bruxelles, 1943), pp. 194–195. Before accepting the crown, Leopold had expressed strong objections to the limited power accorded the head of state by the Constitution of 1830. See HP, II, 62; and Discailles, *Rogier*, III, 228–229.

ficated, now it was necessary not to do anything which would lose the
fine position he had created for Belgium in Europe, a position he
deemed now far in excess of the hopes of 1830.[1]

For all of Leopold's foreboding and the Liberal's impressive-sounding
program,[2] the new cabinet which took office on August 12, 1847, was
far from ideological unanimity. Metternich received correct reports
that the election had really been a victory for a host of local liberal
associations and coalitions and in the last analysis only Rogier (Interior)
and d'Hoffschmidt (Foreign Affairs) were attached to the principles
of moderate liberalism.[3] A month had hardly passed before the minister of war, Chazal, was writing to Rogier strong criticisms of their
minister of public works, the thirty-five year old Frère-Orban.[4]
Rogier had, in fact, had difficulty in getting a number of able liberals
to serve. He received outright refusals from Delfosse, Brouckère and
d'Elhounge, while Veydt, Haussy and Chazal agreed only with reluctance. Health was a common excuse but several believed the king
to be opposed to genuine liberalism and they were reluctant to lend
themselves to a ministry which would be called liberal but which in
fact failed to satisfy all liberal factions. In the opinion of the French
ambassador, the result was a cabinet with a number of mediocre talents,
a ministry of generally humble origins in a state where aristocracy
counted for a great deal.[5]

The campaign leading to the election had been strenuously fought,
with bitterness generated on both sides. As Rogier took office, he
faced two unpleasant episodes which were symptomatic of the intensi-

[1] Leopold to Rogier, July 8, 1847, RP, 107. This letter reproduced in Discailles, *Rogier*,
III, 164. See also Firmin Rogier to Charles Rogier, July 30, 1847 in Discailles, *Rogier*, III,
178–181, reporting Leopold's laudatory remarks in Paris and also his questions about the
opinions of Frère-Orban.

[2] The Liberal program, oriented about the concept of a lay state with a government
enjoying civil independence, can be found in Discailles, *Rogier*, III, 184–186; or in Hymans,
Frère-Orban, I, 175–178, in both cases as it appeared in *Le Moniteur belge* on August 13, 1847.
This published program made a favorable impression within Belgium. See d'Hoffschmidt to
Nothomb, Aug. 20, 1847, AEB, Pr., VIII. For a survey of the liberal program of the Alliance
and the general progress of liberal legislation, see Emile Banning's account in Eugène van
Bemmel, ed., *Patria Belgica* (3 vols., Bruxelles, 1873–1875), II, 491–493.

[3] Lützow to Metternich, June 22, Aug. 16, 31, 1847, AEV. See also Discailles, *Rogier*, III,
147–150; and Rumigny to Guizot, Aug. 16, 1847, AEF, Belg., XXIX. For liberal factions,
see Hymans, *Frère-Orban*, I, 82–88, 98–108; Discailles, *Rogier*, III, 133–137, 145–151; and
especially Louis Bertrand, *Histoire de la démocratie et du socialisme en Belgique depuis 1830*
(2 vols., Bruxelles, 1906–07), I, 214–237, 271. Many liberals were particularly disappointed
with the program.

[4] Chazal to Rogier, Sept. 20, 1847, RP, 126. Other members of the new cabinet were Veydt
(finance) and Haussy (justice).

[5] Rumigny to Guizot, July 31, Aug. 2, 11, 1847, AEF, Belg., XXIX; and Discailles,
Rogier, III, 161–163, 166–167, 169–175.

ty of partisan feeling and of personal reluctance to acquiesce gracefully before the mandate bestowed on the new government.[1] The monarchy's position against the Liberals and the cooperation between the clergy and the Catholic Party combined to heighten further the latent feelings of distrust between the parties and between the Liberals and Leopold. These antagonisms were longstanding and not to disappear readily. In a letter to Metternich, Leopold explained what had happened. As he saw it, a completely unjust reaction had occurred against the Catholics. Unfortunately the bishops had been partial and maladroit and the Catholic majority had been lost, he went on, through intrigues in the larger cities. Ghent had been won by the promise of a direct railroad line, Liège by extensive development of shipping conditions on the Meuse, such appeals as these to private interests had carried the day. In a self-sacrificing flourish the king found his consolation in noting that for seventeen years he had conserved and consolidated "the unique national element" without an instant of hesitation and weakness.[2]

The new ministry's coming to power was followed by a reshuffling of officials. Some changes had been expected, particularly since the Liberals had been put off for so long, but the actual shake-up in domestic offices was decidedly more than usual and made for unfavorable publicity.[3]

The most touchy problem in this area involved the removal of the Civil Governor of Namur, d'Huart, whose sentiments of loyalty were distrusted by Charles Rogier. Though d'Huart had nominally given his support to the ministerial program, he objected strongly to the replacement of some *commissaires d'arrondissement* in his province. Rogier consequently proposed to dismiss him from office but d'Huart "clung to his post with pertinacity." Many were surprised that the governor, a former minister and a forceful independent type of person, would want to stay in office under a minister that he could not work with cordially. Since d'Huart was in favor with the king, the situation

---

[1] Rumigny to Guizot, June 3, 1847, AEF, Belg., XXIX. The diplomatic corps generally was free from such bitterness and major posts continued to be held by most of the same men; an example was the Prince de Ligne in Paris. See the excerpt from his letter to Firmin Rogier, Aug. 6, 1847, in Prince de Ligne, *Souvenirs et Portraits, 1830–1856* (Bruxelles, 1930), pp. 30–31.

[2] Leopold to Metternich, Dec. 31, 1847, AEV.

[3] Walden to Palmerston, Sept. 7, 1847, F.O. 10/133. Four *commissaires d'arrondissement* were put on the pension list superseding seven others, of whom four had their residences changed. Also see RP, 83, for a number of letters and papers regarding the touchy problems of taxing nobility and restricting the transmission of titles; and *La Belgique Judiciaire* (Feb. 10, 1848), pp. 178–191.

became strained. Leopold supported him but constitutional right and precedent were on Rogier's side. Finally the issue was bluntly put to Leopold – he must choose between d'Huart and the government. When the question was put in this context, Leopold grudgingly saw d'Huart replaced by Vrière, then Belgium's *chargé d'affaires* in Portugal. Rogier noted a similarity between Leopold's actions in this incident and the practices of his father-in-law, Louis Philippe.[1]

Awkward as the episode over d'Huart was, it had a more embarrassing parallel on the international scene in the matter of Belgium's diplomatic representation at Rome. The preceding government, really out of office after June 12 but still serving in a care-taker capacity, appointed Count Van der Straeten de Ponthoz to represent Belgian interests in Rome after a temporary mission by the Prince de Chimay had expired. This late selection caused considerable surprise. It gave the appearance of being an extension of the recent bitter electoral campaign since Van der Straeten was a decided partisan of the Catholic Party and the clergy had been very active in the campaign. It was even interpreted in the Chamber of Deputies (by Le Hon on November 19) as an attempt by the Catholic Party to make Rome think that they had not really been beaten in the elections. The appointment was at once attacked by the Liberals and, upon taking office, they cancelled it and proposed instead the attorney-general of the court of appeals, Mathieu Leclercq. Again Leopold was ranged against the government, but eventually and with reluctance, he signed the decree appointing Leclercq. His language referring to the incident during his Speech from the Throne on November 9 convinced Rogier further that the king genuinely approved the *ad interim* action of the earlier ministry. In Rome the Holy See objected to the appointment of Leclercq for reasons still obscure. It may have been because of Leclercq's known opposition to the idea of Papal supremacy in the Belgian church. There had been considerable passion aroused against the church in the previous elections and the objection to Leclercq now looked like outside clerical interference in the selection of a Belgian official. Initially, Papal opposition amazed Rogier and his colleagues because the new Pope was himself understood to have liberal sentiments. The ministry at once hardened its position and refused to appoint anybody else. The government construed the Papal objection to be simply an attempt at retali-

---

[1] Walden to Palmerston, Nov. 6, 13, 1847, F.O. 10/133. See also *l'Indépendance belge*, Nov. 5, 1847; and Rumigny to Guizot, Oct. 29, Nov. 3, 1847, AEF, Belg. XXIX. For a more detailed account, see Discailles, *Rogier*, III, 211–217. There was no personal opposition by Leopold to Vrière, a close associate of Van Praet's.

ation by Belgium's Catholic Party which was still licking its wounds. The situation was further complicated by Leclercq's unwillingness to accept the appointment if the Pope extended anything less than full acceptance of him as an envoy. Actually, the Pope was thought to be willing to receive Leclercq personally though the formal objections would remain. At length when the Papacy gave way to this extent, Leclercq firmly refused to compromise. The whole issue appears meshed in Belgian politics. It was not a constitutional problem or even a matter of international friction based on anything more than personalities. Rome's opposition was never specific. It was in general terms and negative; Leclercq simply did not possess those qualities the Papal government wanted to see in a Belgian representative. Leclercq had been the minister of justice in the Lebeau cabinet in 1840 and was regarded as a dedicated Catholic and a man of integrity. In politics his liberalism was moderate. Rather than it being a genuine rejection of Leclercq because of his personal qualities, it more likely was disappointment over seeing Van der Straeten replaced. There was also perhaps the additional factor that Van der Straeten's ambitions for some time had focussed on securing this appointment. At any rate, as with d'Huart, there could be no question about the legality of the government's position. Public sentiment was such that when Rogier forced a vote in the Chamber on the question, the result favored the ministry by 95 to 1, indicating the *public* adhesion of the Catholic Party and the strength of public opinion.[1]

For a short time in September Leopold seemed reconciled to the new government and to realize that another Catholic government simply was not possible. Earlier the cabinet had been irritated at an attitude ascribed to Leopold. In addition to his known views on constitutional government, he had lived somewhat in seclusion and retirement and this was interpreted by all parties as indicating at least indifference and perhaps even contempt. He now became more active in public to the relief of everyone. Leopold recognized and seemed to accept the idea that there was wide-spread support for the Liberals, a fact that had been especially dramatized by Chazal's appointment as war

[1] Walden to Palmerston, Sept. 28, Oct. 2, 19, Nov. 13, 16, 20, 23, 1847, F.O. 10/133. See especially *l'Indépendance belge*, Oct. 1, 1847, for the government's view; also HP, II, 603–604 606, 610–611, 675; letters of Sept.–Nov., 1847, RP, 83; Lützow to Metternich, June 22, 1847, AEV; and Hymans, *Frère-Orban*, I, 167. The post remained vacant until the appointment of the Prince de Ligne. See Ligne, *Souvenirs*, pp. 87–124; and Discailles, *Rogier*, III, 183, 201–206, 272. Discailles notes (III, 206, 215) that J. J. Thonissen, *La Belgique sous le règne de Léopold Ier* (4 vols., 1855–58, Liège) fails to mention either the Leclercq or d'Huart incidents, nor the earlier two-month ministerial crisis.

minister. This was greeted with wholesale enthusiasm by an army overwhelmingly liberal in sentiment. Unfortunately, the effect of the d'Huart and Van der Straeten incidents was to strain severely the relations of the ministry with the king. Leopold had even been cordial with particular cabinet members and he was understood as wanting to see the emergence of a new party that would unite the most moderate of the Liberals with the most liberal of the Catholics. The early friction over appointments doomed this for when Rogier felt that the crown opposed him, he looked more to extreme liberals for support than he had originally intended. Early impressions were that the government was weak but the final acquiescence of Leopold in the appointments questions and the Catholic support in the Chamber when a stand had to be taken in public were clear indications to the contrary.[1]

While the government's legal position was thus demonstrated to be strong, the gap between it and the nation's monarch was very real and subject to aggravation. This was clear in debates over a request by d'Hoffschmidt for supplementary credits for his office in connection with expenses incurred through past decorations – particularly the Order of Leopold. These had been given quite lavishly, many of them to foreigners. The debate stressed the number of foreigners so-honored with d'Hoffschmidt arguing that while the need to cut costs was obvious and desired, nevertheless the decorations were justified as part of Belgium's diplomacy since 1830. A number of former ministers were reproached in the debate though finally, on January 25, 1848, the credits were voted by a margin of 34 to 28. In the guise of the government defending the need for credits, the previous ministers and Leopold himself were criticized. It was known that Leopold had a strong voice in selecting foreigners for the award and the strength of the publicized report clearly showed a thinness of mutual confidence.[2]

The reports sent home by the British ambassador to Belgium, Howard de Walden and Seaford, were largely matter-of-fact accounts of activities and attitudes as he discerned them in Brussels. He found the new government operating well within strictly defined constitutional practice and suggested that too much was perhaps being made of the frictions between the cabinet and king over appointments. He professed

[1] Walden to Palmerston, Sept. 23, Nov. 13, 16, 1847, F.O. 10/133. Also Rumigny to Guizot, Sept. 15, 1847, Jan. 22, 1848, AEF, Belg. XXIX. Rumigny reported that d'Hoffschmidt was the minister held in the highest regard by Leopold.

[2] Walden to Palmerston, Dec. 18, 1847, F.O. 10/133; and HP, II, 611–612, 659–660.

to see nothing "in either the acts or tone of the government to warrant the slightest apprehensions as to the tendency to any dangerous policy" but noted that Rogier's ministry was "peculiarly unpalatable" to the French embassy at Brussels.[1]

---

[1] Walden to Palmerston, Sept. 23, Nov. 6, 13, 1847, F.O. 10/133. The Belgian correspondent of *The Economist*, Jan. 8, 1848, maintained that the clerical influence was modest and by crying out against it, the government was resorting to "worn out questions, which belong to a bygone century." It should abandon this "struggle against a phantom" and turn its energies into objects more becoming the reign of the middle classes.

CHAPTER II

DOMESTIC PROBLEMS

The Liberals had assumed responsibility for the conduct of affairs in a year when bountiful harvests were reversing the spiral of prices.[1] This welcome abundance, after two bad years, was noted on November 9, 1847, by Leopold in his Speech from the Throne to the combined Senate and Chamber of Deputies. He emphasized the importance of agriculture in the Belgian economy; it deserved an honored place on a par with industry, a relationship he would soon dramatize by establishing awards for outstanding workers in these noble careers. In the contexts of calling for more public works and for penal reform, the king mentioned the extreme poverty and widespread pauperism still in Flanders.[2] Famous for linens and flourishing for centuries, Flanders was in dire straits progressively after 1836 when changes in manufacturing techniques in Great Britain spelled the end of Flemish prosperity.[3] Pauperism was understood to be the sad but inevitable accompaniment to industry, an indictment against the whole process of industrialization. Rogier, indeed, saw the situation as a compelling challenge, not only for the Liberals but for civilization itself.[4] Rogier, Chazal, Van Praet, and a number of other important Belgians were strongly influenced by the ideas of Saint-Simon and Fourier. An effective program was thus expected to alleviate conditions in Flanders

[1] Walden to Palmerston, September 7, 1847, F.O. 10/133.

[2] HP, II, 603–604.

[3] *The Economist*, Feb. 26, 1848.

[4] Henry-Thierry Deschamps, *La Belgique devant la France; l'opinion et l'attitude françaises de 1839 à 1848* (Paris, 1956), pp. 518–520. For a series of relevant penetrating studies, see *Revue du Nord*, XXXVIII, (Jan.–Mar., 1956): F. Lentacker, "Les ouvriers belges dans le département du Nord au milieu du XIXe siècle," 5–14; M. Gillet, "Aspects de la crise de 1846–1851 dans le bassin houiller du Nord," 15–27; F. P. Codaccioni, "Le textile lillois devant la crise 1846–1851," 29–63; L. Machu, "La crise de l'industrie textile à Roubaix au milieu du XIXe siècle," 65–75; and A. Chanut, "La crise économique à Tourcoing (1846–1850)," 77–105. These five authors have also combined their efforts in a particularly fine analysis, "Aspects industriels de la crise: Le Département du Nord" in E. Labrousse, ed., *Aspects de la crise et de la dépression de l'économie française au milieu du XIXe siècle 1846–1851* (*Bibliothèque de la Révolution de 1848*, Tome XIX), La Roche-sur-Yon, 1956, 93–141.

and Leopold supported such a hope as he informed Rogier in this context that his counted on his zeal.[1]

Leopold had hardly stopped praising the Belgian economy when it took a turn for the worse. The commercial crisis in Britain had little effect in Belgium but by November 26, the situation became grave. Payments were suspended by several firms in Antwerp, Ghent and Brussels, including two of the largest in the nation. At Mons only immediate aid could have kept up employment and the government became gravely concerned, the minister of finances turning to the Société Générale and to Rothschild. However, both of these would make advances only on sound treasury bonds and the treasury itself was empty.[2] The government was unable to intervene and two of the largest firms in Mons suspended payments. This financial embarrassment was judged by the French ambassador to be an important factor in the planned resignation of the finance minister.[3] Meanwhile, news of "grands sinistres commerciaux" at Frankfort and elsewhere, sadness at the pallace following the death of Louis Philippe's sister, Adelaide, as well as pessimistic word from London, all added up to a sad beginning for the New Year of 1848 and the French ambassador wrote that he sensed a sort of terror in the air.[4] There were thus in Belgium a host of grave social problems, so readily discerned that the Austrian ambassador had called Metternich's attention to the chance to study them easily. It was, he believed, a fine opportunity to derive distinct analyses of problems which existed elsewhere but in not so handy a form. They could perhaps have worked themselves out without dangerous repercussions but for this peace was necessary in Europe – and this was to be at a premium.[5]

Leopold had also praised the army which he called brave and well-organized. Only eight days later, however, it was the subject of inquiry as the deputy from Tournai questioned, among other things, whether the construction of new fortresses wasn't an anachronism. Chazal replied that he had no intention of making Belgium a massive fortress and that he was in fact about to name a commission to study

---

[1] Bertrand, *Démocratie*, I, 96–137, 194–195; and Discailles, *Rogier*, III, 218–221.

[2] Rumigny to Guizot, Oct. 29, Nov. 6, 26, 1847, AEF, Belg., XXIX; and *The Economist*, Jan. 1, 22, 1848. For general course of Belgian industrialization from 1830 to 1850 and especially the roles of the Société Générale and the Rothschilds, see Rondo Cameron, *France and the Economic Development of Europe 1800–1914* (Princeton, 1961), pp. 119–125, 336–361.

[3] Rumigny to Guizot, Dec. 3, 19, 1847, AEF, Belg., XXIX, Though Veydt planned to retire early in 1848, because of the crisis in February, he agreed to stay on and his retirement was delayed until May, 1848.

[4] Rumigny to Guizot, Jan. 3, 1848, *ibid.*

[5] Woyna to Metternich, May 15, 1847, AEV.

the whole question of the best means of assuring the defense of the kingdom. The investigation was to compare particularly the effectiveness of the various fortresses, considering possible costs of demolition as well as maintenance.[1]

These problems of defense and Flemish poverty met in a third consideration, the budget. The three became consuming interests for Rogier and his colleagues and were already of major importance before complicated by the social, political, military, and economic ramifications of the February Revolution in France.[2]

The budgets for various sections of the government were soon to be severely strained by abnormal burdens. In early August, 1848, when d'Hoffschmidt needed more funds and asked Haussy, the minister of justice, if he could use some of his, he was refused on the grounds that these funds too were nearly expended. An earlier request for supplemental funds for the ministry of foreign affairs had easily met approval but this was within days of the revolt in Paris when anything regarding the safety of the kingdom was given a high priority.[3]

In the December debates (1847) on the army budget, Chazal argued that the army was already at a minimum and that further cuts would render it ineffective. The army then stood at about 32,600 men though these figures were deceptive since at short notice nearly 80,000 could be mustered. Its size had been tentatively established by law (May 8, 1847) at a maximum of 70,000 men but one deputy, Osy, thought on December 10 that this number could be reduced to 60,000. By the 29th, he was maintaining that an army of 26,000 was enough for peacetime defense. Interest in the matter was high because it involved new taxes. Chazal won important support by showing that, despite its precarious geographic position, Belgium spent less on its military establishment than either Holland or Bavaria. At the same time he stressed that he would never refuse any economy so long as it was consistent with good organization and he suggested three prospective economies of a moderate sort regarding rations. Persons demanding savings at the same time wanted an army as strong as possible in wartime and as little onerous as possible in peacetime. All fortresses not indispensable to the defense

---

[1] HP, II, 606; and Walden to Palmerston, Nov. 27, 1847, F.O. 10/133. On another level Chazal was concerned about what could be done to promote liberalism in the army; see Chazal to Rogier, Sept. 20, 1847, RP, 126.

[2] In 1847 revenue (115, 336, 650 fr.) exceeded expenditures (114, 280, 975 fr.). In 1846 there was an imbalance of imports (224,400,000 fr.) over exports (183,000,000 fr.). See Walden to Palmerston, Feb. 1, 1848, and accompanying memo, F.O. 10/137.

[3] D'Hoffschmidt to Haussy, Aug. 1, 5, 1848, and Haussy to d'Hoffschmidt, Aug. 7, 1848, DM, V; and HP, II, 677.

of the nation ought to be torn down. In the Senate Chazal met similar complaints by again showing that the army was organized more efficiently than foreign armies. Some senators thought that the army budget could be alleviated by more reliance on the civic guard. This revealed further dissension since the civic guard was unpopular and attempts at organization had failed in a number of places, particularly Antwerp. Rogier argued that the civic guard was a separate issue to be discussed later. He insisted that an increased and fully organized guard could not be regarded, even if it existed, and it not did, as a substitute for an effective army. The debates on the civic guard came in late April and early May, 1848, when there was support for a strong defensive force and the issues were less fundamental than they would have been had the discussions occurred in a time free from the threat of invasion.[1]

Earlier in April, 1848, the war department had needed both a supplementary and an extraordinary credit. The discussions took place in an atmosphere of praise for the army, for Chazal and measures he had taken, and of gratitude for the success in repelling invasion at Risquons -Tout. Senators and deputies that usually lined up on the side of economy in the military budget now supported the emergency measures in terms of enthusiastic approval for Chazal. Delfosse in the Chamber declared his approval for the credit because of the enormous responsibility then resting on the government when a single day of disorder, invasion, or anarchy could mean the ruin of the country. He made it clear, however, that he believed a number of economies could have been instituted.

One strong voice of criticism did appear. In the Chamber Adelson Castiau eloquently opposed such armaments as a useless luxury. He saw no menace from France; it had even been France in 1831 that had saved Belgium. There was nothing to fear from Germany where "the holy alliance of peoples has replaced the holy alliance of kings." As for the recent armed bands, the civic guard could maintain order. After all, two hundred men had been enough to repel them and without much bloodshed. Castiau especially regretted the raids because they hurt the republican cause which he favored. He believed earnestly that a republican government, legally and peacefully established in Brussels would best guarantee nationality, independence, liberty, and order for

---

[1] HP, II, 640–642, 681–687; Woyna to Metternich, May 15, 1847, AEV; and Walden to Palmerston, Feb. 1, 1848 and accompanying memo, F.O. 10/137. The French ambassador even had praise for Chazal's remarks. See Rumigny to Guizot, Dec. 31, 1847, AEF, Belg., XXIX.

Belgium. Such marked opposition of views regarding the form of government led him to retire from office on April 5. Responding to Castiau's arguments, Rogier maintained that support of the army was essential to protect the institutions of the nation. Other efforts against the measures from some papers "Belgian only in name" were dismissed as not appropriate subjects for discussion and the credits were voted overwhelmingly. In the general discussion later in July, there was little support for the subject of army reductions as suggested in late June by Senator de Royer who saw it as a safe possibility since, in his view, calm was being reestablished in Europe.[1]

Appropriations to do something about pauperism in Flanders were readily passed by the two houses as the debates centered on the extent of aid and the form it should take. Many senators, Dumon-Dumortier among them, felt that thus far all attempts to help Flanders had really been only a matter of modest palliatives. A more comprehensive approach was needed to the problem. To begin with, the dole should be replaced by work and if work could not be created, then some of the population should be moved to places where workers were needed or work could be made. Rogier's initial requests for what he called the most urgent needs were criticized as insufficient and not a sharp enough break with former practice. Indeed, on December 20, 1847, Senator de Ribaucourt declared that the ministry had done nothing so far to relieve the situation in Flanders. Rogier had set up within the ministry of the interior a bureau spécial for Flemish affairs to make studies and suggest specific remedies and he responded that a series of measures had already been taken. In fact, however, a specific practical program was not placed before the Chamber until March 28, 1848.[2]

The "issue" of Flemish poverty continued to be an embarrassment to the government. Rogier's ministry was accused (Jan.-Feb., 1849) of using the occasion of the February Revolution in Paris as an excuse to forget its campaign promises. Rogier's responses that the government was doing all it could and actually making headway were unconvincing.[3] This must, however, be seen in the context of the ineffective

---

[1] HP, II, 643-644, 690-961, 703-704, 712-713; and Hymans, *Frère-Orban*, I, 230. Chazal declared that horses good enough for cavalry use were hard to find. For a sketch of Adelson's career, see Bertrand, *Démocratie*, I, 238-250.

[2] HP, II, 627-628, 674, 680; and Discailles, *Rogier*, III, 190-191. Rogier pointed to some clearings of heaths, local road improvements, creation of some model workshops, and plans for a school for ship cabin boys.

[3] HP, II, 728-729. He was criticized in *The Economist*, Jan. 15, 1848, for supporting fixed duties on corn to protect agriculture rather than applying free trade principles. His liberalism was also suspect because of his support of government intervention in many areas.

Catholic view of the problem which saw pauperism as evoking sympathy and charity. Charity was religious in essence and not something to be regimented or interfered with. Thus the Catholic answer to pauperism was charity based on freedom of giving.[1]

The need for action was all the more serious because of a "great increase of a malignant fever of a Typhoid nature" and a medical commission was dispatched to suggest practical remedies. Meanwhile, the medical officers in regiments quartered in Flanders were doing what they could but both the poor and those trying to save them were alike succumbing to disease.[2] A number of people, ranging socially from town-dwellers to the king, thought of colonization and emigration as a way of dealing with the over-population problem. Petitions, commissions, and inquiries all bore no fruit as 1848 was too highly volatile for a new colonial program to be easily instituted.[3] Another dimension to the problem of government aid for Flanders was the smouldering ill-will felt in some areas over the fact that the new ministry was heavily Walloon in character, only Veydt from Antwerp was Flemish. This made it all the easier to declare that half-measures simply were the result of a lack of concern.[4]

After the revolution in Paris, the unfortunate situation in Flanders became only part of the unemployment problem. The government turned to extensive public works as a basic key to stability. At all costs more employment had to be found and work stoppages were closely watched. The government was forced to revise its needs radically and its requests for funds from the Chamber and Senate became both frequent and substantial. A genuine crisis was developing in the area of finance as the earlier situation in Flanders became only part of a national problem of indigence and need. Publicly, however, Leopold noted that the treasury was in good shape.[5]

The government tried to alleviate the unemployment problem in two particular areas, the building of canals and railroads. After heated debate on the various proposals, appropriate credits were made available as there was agreement to Frère-Orban's observation that the real

---

[1] The idea of an exposition of Flemish arts and industry was ridiculed by Catholics as being no help whatever. Leopold opened the exposition on Sept. 24, 1847. See Discailles, *Rogier*, III, 194–195; and Hymans, *Frère-Orban*, I, 506–515.

[2] Waller to Palmerston, Feb. 12, 1848, F.O. 10/137.

[3] HP, II, 716. See also "Emigration et colonisation: Aperçu des projets et des essais antérieurs au moment actuel," AEB, Emigration et Colonisation (2030); and Walden to Palmerston, Jan. 26, 1848, F.O. 10/137.

[4] Lützow to Metternich, Aug. 16, 1847, AEV.

[5] HP, II, 644, 701; and E. Conway to Van de Weyer, Mar. 11, 1848, VWP, 172.

issue was that men be kept working rather than the pros and cons of particular projects.[1] So long as people were working and making enough to live, the forces of disorder could be controlled.

[1] HP, II, 664–666, 677–679. Part of the difficulty in getting support for rail construction projects stemmed from known defects in existing railway administration resulting in excessive costs for operation. Frère-Orban was also instrumental in postal reform. See *The Economist*, Jan. 29, 1848; and Hymans, *Frère-Orban*, I, 186–194, 212–222.

CHAPTER III

BELGIUM IN EUROPEAN DIPLOMACY PRIOR TO FEBRUARY, 1848

The general appearance of stability in Europe in 1847 had its exceptions which created dissension and distrust. The intrigue and maneuvering over the Spanish marriages had recently embittered international relations and Stockmar wrote trenchantly in August that "Louis Philippe's reputation as a master of the arts of statesmanship has been most unequivocally ruined by the Spanish intrigue. If he lives long enough, he can hardly fail to suffer some portion of the punishment, which, according to the laws of nature, he has incurred." [1]

Within France the new British ambassador, Normanby, had followed (January, 1847) a course open to criticism on a number of grounds. With Palmerston's concurrence he had been showing important papers to both Molé and Thiers so that these opponents of Guizot could be more damaging in their attacks in the Chamber. This relationship was common knowledge among diplomats in Paris and Guizot, understandably indignant, had adopted an attitude of cold formality towards Normanby. [2]

Political discussion in France early in the year centered on the prospects of Thiers in his rivalry with Guizot. The stability of the monarchy itself was not in doubt. Specifically on this subject Leopold of Belgium observed from the Tuileries that "France... has already been *under water several times, what could be spoiled has been spoiled, what remains is pretty solid.*" [3] Sir Edward Blount later recalled that

[1] Stockmar to [Albert], Aug. 1, 1847, in Theodore Martin, *Life of the Prince Consort* (4 vols., New York, 1875–1879), II, 13. See also Victoria to Leopold, Sept. 7, 1847, LV, II, 151–152.

[2] Charles F. G. Greville, *The Greville Memoirs 1814–1860* (8 vols. London, 1938), V, 383, 393, 403, 408. The "most imprudent" Madame de Lieven was especially vocal, condemning many of Normanby's actions and his "asking advice of different people, and very incompetent people too."

[3] Leopold to Victoria, Jan. 15, 1847, LV, II, 138–139; and Ligne, *Souvenirs*, pp. 60–61. Indeed, Louis Philippe had even been advising Leopold to beware of the activities of liberal associations which he equated to the clubs of Paris. Leopold appears to have regarded the danger of liberal associations as stemming from the disapproval their actions might prompt

"No throne in Europe was, to all outward appearances, more secure in 1847 than that of Louis Philippe." [1] Louis Blanc noted that many people were reacting to suggestions of possible revolution with a skeptical smile and the assurance that if it came, it would be after Louis Philippe's time. Lamartine was in this general category.[2]

Throughout 1847 most of the great powers were in continual correspondence regarding insurrections and instability in Switzerland. In Brussels the foreign ministry was kept *au courant* by its various ambassadors as material in the archives of the ministry today testifies.[3] Leopold was in direct touch with Metternich on the Swiss problem and declared himself saddened by word of radical success in Switzerland. He saw hope in Austria's position which he characterized as strong and solidly based, a real guarantee of European stability. The French Jacobin spirit, then being promoted by Palmerston, was the great menace which could denationalize the masses and threatened all thrones and governments.[4]

Like other monarchs of his day Leopold practiced private diplomacy. In October he was visiting with his father-in-law, Louis Philippe, at Saint-Cloud. Through Jules Van Praet, his household minister, Leopold inquired about the details of Britain's financial crisis, passing word to the Belgian embassy in London that financiers in Paris would like to see Peel at the head of affairs.[5] His correspondence in November included a letter from Metternich which discussed the current dangers in Europe and specifically analyzed the problems of Italy.[6] His closeness to both the French monarch and the British crown encouraged all kinds of rumors – such as one that, Louis Philippe, having first obtained Metternich's consent and support, was going to send Leopold to London to get the British ministry not to oppose the occupation of Rome by French troops.[7] A small advantage for Belgium that flowed from

from Belgium's neighbors. A democratic regime, he noted, might be feasible if Belgium had neighbors with whom she had to stay on reasonable terms. See Discailles, *Rogier*, III, 136, 177–178, 182; and Bertrand, *Démocratie*, I, 229–231.

[1] Edward Blount, *Memoirs of Sir Edward Blount* (London, 1902), p. 111.

[2] Louis Blanc, *Pages d'Histoire de la Révolution de Février* (Paris, 1850), pp. 4, 27. See especially Paul Thureau-Dangin, *Histoire de la monarchie de juillet* (7 vols., Paris, 1884–1892), VII, for a survey of French foreign and domestic history in 1847.

[3] See for example Nothomb to d'Hoffschmidt, Nov. 9, 10, 11, 15, 21, 23, 27, Dec. 8, 14, 1847, Jan. 6, 9, 11 (2 letters), 13, 15, 20, 23, Feb. 11, 1848, AEB, Pr., VIII.

[4] Woyna to Metternich, Dec. 6, 1847; and Leopold to Metternich, Dec. 31, 1847, AEV.

[5] Van Praet to Van de Weyer, Oct. 12, 1847, VWP, 274.

[6] Metternich to Leopold, Nov. 24, 1847, AEV.

[7] Woyna to Metternich, Jan. 26, 1848, *ibid*. As well as being Louis Philippe's son-in-law, Leopold was also, of course, an uncle to *both* Queen Victoria and Prince Albert.

Leopold's family connections was the replacement of Belgian laces for Norman at the court of Louis Philippe.[1]

While concerned about British economic difficulties, Leopold slowly sensed the danger developing within France. The King of the Belgians wrote on January 12, 1848, that "bad passions" were being kept in check by Louis Philippe but a month later he was not so confident.[2] Peel saw signs of "an immediate revolution" [3] and Prussia's envoy in Paris, Baron d'Arnim, was predicting the government's fall.[4] "Louis Philippe, in spite of the menacing signs of the times and the ill-concealed alarm of his own Court, was not be persuaded that there was any real danger." [5] He had a high regard for his own abilities and thought he was popular with the French public.[6] Feeling secure with a confidence that proved misplaced, Louis Philippe declared that he was so firmly in the saddle that "neither banquets of cold veal nor Bonaparte" could throw him from his horse.[7] The bourgeois king had a stubborn streak that, to his misfortune, increased with age and made him progressively more difficult to influence. Sir John Bowring believed that only the monarch's sister, Adelaide, had any influence over him. Cavendish attributes Louis Philippe's mistakes in February, 1848, as being largely due to the shock of losing Adelaide.[8]

In Great Britain while some recognized that "the revolutionary spirit" existed in Paris and were uneasy over its potentiality, yet this apprehension had not reached the point where there was fear that the Orleans dynasty was in danger.[9] While Guizot's hostility was being courted earlier by Normanby, at the same time in Paris Greville wrote

---

[1] Michelle Perrot, "Aspects Industriels de la crise: Les Régions Textiles du Calvados," p. 165, in Labrousse, *Aspects*, pp. 164–199.

[2] Leopold to Victoria, Jan. 12, Feb. 12, 1848, LV, II, 173–175. In January of 1848, Leopold and his Queen spent time in both Paris and London. See Walden to Palmerston, Jan. 4, 11, 15, 22, 1848, F.O. 10/137.

[3] Blount, *Memoirs*, p. 110.

[4] Woyna to Metternich, Jan. 13, 1848, AEV.

[5] Blount, *Memoirs*, p. 113.

[6] John Bowring, *Autobiographical Recollections of Sir John Bowring* (London, 1877), pp. 261, 263.

[7] Quoted in Carlo Bronne, *Leopold Ier et son temps* (Bruxelles, 1947), p. 221; and in Bertrand, *Démocratie*, I, 275. Guizot and Duchâtel also felt there was no danger (Blount, *Memoirs*, p. 110). However, his health was bad and it was reported that a number of conservatives were exploring means leading to abdication; see *The Economist*, Jan. 22, 1848.

[8] Bowring, *Recollections*, pp. 264–265, and Francis W. H. Cavendish, *Society, Politics and Diplomacy 1820–1864: Passages from the Journal of Francis W. H. Cavendish* (London, 1913), p. 142 (Mar.2, 1848) and also Leopold to Victoria, Jan. 1, 1848, LV, II, 168. Louis Blanc attributed the revolution to being the fruits of years of corruption; see Blanc, *Pages*, pp. 2–9; also *The Economist*, Feb. 26, 1848, for another indictment of corruption.

[9] Cavendish, *Journal*, pp. 138–139 (Feb. 19, 1848). See also *The Economist*, Feb. 19, 1848, for yet another writer that reported serious unrest and was uncertain that Louis Philippe's government would be "strong enough to repel a general bursting out of public opinion."

his estimate although "we are in danger of cutting a contemptible figure" nevertheless "nothing can be so impolitic as to create a belief here that the people of England are resolved to submit to anything rather than go to war." [1] Through 1847 there was a developing hostility on the continent to Britain's support of movements for reform and constitutional guarantees. In September Victoria wrote to Leopold of Belgium that the "state of politics is very critical" and the future seemed to be one that could only justify present anxiety.[2]

In January of 1848 Leopold received a report from the Belgian ambassador in London, Van de Weyer, detailing a number of points at which the British were in active opposition to the interests of a number of continental powers. Palmerston was the object of bitter attacks in Paris and his conduct during the Swiss question particularly infuriated the French. On the other hand, Palmerston believed that Guizot was trying to use a segment of the British press to undermine his (Palmerston's) personal position in the cabinet and at court.[3] Suspicion and sullen hostility entered an alarmingly serious phase when Wellington informed John Burgoyne that the entire southern coast was vulnerable to invasion. This had been intended as a confidential estimate but word leaked out and tensions increased.[4] Also symptomatic of deteriorating relations were John Russell's slighting remarks on February 18 "in a style far from judicious" in reference to France and her military establishment.[5] On the continent plans were developing for an alliance between Russia, Austria, Prussia, and France. These powers had agreed that British intrigue must be met by some sort of concrete measures, particularly in the light of events in Spain, Portugal, Switzerland, and Italy. Indeed, March 15, 1848, had been set as the date when the arrangements were to be settled.[6] This threatening situation was drastically altered, of course, by the February Revolution as, to use Carlo Bronne's trenchant phrase, destiny turned the page.[7]

Through the maze of conflicting national and dynastic aims and intrigues, Leopold moved with a kind of facility which was unique.

[1] Greville, *Memoirs*, V, 403.

[2] Victoria to Leopold, Sept. 7, 1847, LV, II, 151–152.

[3] Van de Weyer to Leopold, Jan. 17, 1848, VWP, 116. At the same time Guizot suspected that, in turn, the Prussian envoy, Baron d'Arnim, was intriguing with his (Guizot's) political opposition, as Normanby had earlier; see Woyna to Metternich, Jan. 13, 1848, AEV.

[4] Martin, *Consort*, II, 14–15. For details on this whole episode and a running commentary, see *The Economist*, Jan. 1, 8, 22, 29, Feb. 5, 19, 1848.

[6] Greville, *Memoirs*, VI, 16.

[5] Martin, *Consort*, II, 14–15.

[7] Bronne, *Leopold*, p. 223.

His family connections made him an especially important diplomatic figure. Count Woyna, the Austrian ambassador in Brussels, reported to Metternich that Leopold alone enjoyed real influence at both Paris and London. On many occasions Leopold had discussed general European problems freely with Woyna, comparing how they looked from Paris, London, and Central Europe. Woyna said he had tried to keep Leopold well-informed on Swiss problems and insisted that it was essential that he really understand Austria's position, especially regarding Switzerland and Italy. Leopold was advising that in her circumstances Austria could not be too forceful – she must be strong and energetic.[1]

Leopold was, indeed, the perfect intermediary. Though related to the crowns of Britain and France, though well versed in the history of both states and speaking their languages with fluency, he was still a Coburg and his speech revealed a Germanic phraseology – even when speaking in French or English – showing that he thought in German. "Even at his table, German was the accepted and preferred tongue, unless when courtesy to guests, or diplomatic usages made the employment of French or English more becoming." [2] His personal actions and advice often took forms really more related to family relations than to diplomacy as such. A case in point would be his advice to Victoria to drop a note to Louis Philippe regarding Adelaide's death. She wrote the letter after Lord John Russell agreed to the wisdom of her following her "own kind impulse to write a letter to the King of the French." Leopold thanked her for writing the note which he declared had been kissed tenderly by Louis Philippe. Such familiarity with other heads of state, though often trivial, could be of enough importance to cause jealousy and ill-will within the cabinet at Brussels where Leopold was suspected of exceeding his authority.[3] Though there were many things that Leopold could do on his own initiative, he was not really in charge of policy-making in foreign affairs while the Liberals were in office. This was obvious to the Austrian ambassador who reported as much when he noted that Leopold would be unable to take over the reins of government until radicalism (liberalism) had been erased.[4] Nevertheless Woyna believed that Leopold, despite

---

[1] Woyna to Metternich, Dec. 6, 1847, Jan. 13, 1848, AEV.

[2] Bowring, *Recollections*, p. 269–270.

[3] Leopold to Victoria, Jan. 1, 3, 12, 1848; John Russell to Victoria, Jan. 4, 1848; Victoria to Louis Philippe, Jan. 5, 1848; and Louis Philippe to Victoria, Jan. 8, 1848, LV, II, 168–174.

[4] Woyna to Metternich, Jan. 13, 1848, AEV. Leopold had enjoyed unusual power under the earlier ministries of Van de Weyer and Nothomb.

constitutional limitations, was the most important person in Belgium. The sons of the great Belgian families he regarded as insignificant. The views of ministers were consulted by foreign missions simply as a matter of formality – the main job for an ambassador in Brussels was to keep informed somehow on the ideas and intentions of Leopold. This could be done either directly or through Van Praet. Woyna noted that most of the diplomats assigned to Brussels were new there and did not really understand their task – especially in a situation where ministries could change fairly often. Leopold had really accomplished a great deal considering Belgium's precarious geographic situation in Europe. Here Leopold's European outlook had a very distinct asset as well as his support of a strong army. While the social crisis was real, yet, Woyna observed, the banner of communism had yet to be held in a Belgian hand. While there were forces for change, there were also forces for stability. Despite dangerous theories in some of the towns, the priests and the church were still regarded as a pious moral force and there would probably be little that was new in the liberal way of doing things.[1] Woyna was, indeed, quite optimistic.

The outcome of the Belgian elections in 1847 seemed as disagreeable to the government in Paris as it was to Leopold. The French ambassador in Brussels, Rumigny, informed Guizot of the distressing results and while speculation was rife about the new government, he had a favorable word only for d'Hoffschmidt. He judged that while d'Hoffschmidt would accept whatever was offered to him, he would be equally able in foreign affairs, finances, or public works. Otherwise he felt that the ministry generally was composed of "signal mediocrities" and that virtually all men of value in the Liberal Party had refused to join.[2] Austria's embassy was also relaying word to Metternich that a number in the cabinet were new men and that of the Liberal ministry only Rogier and d'Hoffschmidt had had important political experience.[3] Rumigny even questioned whether Rogier exercised much leadership among the liberals. He believed that most impartial observers viewed the cabinet unfavorably and regarded initiative as flowing from Frère-Orban and Haussy within the ministry and from Piercot, an author from Liège, rather than Charles Rogier.[4]

Rumigny's favorable impression of d'Hoffschmidt was further

---

[1] Woyna to Metternich, May 15, 1847, Jan. 13, 1848, *ibid.* Woyna served in Brussels over two years.
[2] Rumigny to Guizot, June 10, July 31, Aug. 2, 11, 1847, AEF, Belg., XXIX.
[3] Lützow to Metternich, Aug. 16, 1847, AEV.
[4] Rumigny to Guizot, Aug. 16, 1847, AEF, Belg., XXIX.

enhanced when he found the new Belgian foreign minister informally
admitting to him that he was a novice, thus creating an atmosphere
where it seemed perfectly natural that Rumigny indulge in giving him
advice. He seized the chance, tellling d'Hoffschmidt that as the only
true moderate in the new cabinet, a great deal depended on how he
created confidence abroad. He spoke of the friendly disposition of
France for Belgium and that in turn France deserved Belgium's trust
and confidence. Above all, he cautioned against the efforts that others
might make to get the Belgians to believe that the French were hoping
to exert undue influence on Belgian domestic and foreign policies.[1]

Whatever confidence or relief Rumigny may have felt about d'Hoffschmidt [2] was in contrast to the apprehensions he reported regarding
Chazal's activities. There seemed to be on the part of the minister of
war, according to the French ambassador, an "extraordinary tendency" to stir up the country to the fear of an attack by a foreign power –
thus necessitating the adoption of defense measures to maintain
Belgian neutrality. Was this motivated by fear of French hostility?
Chazal had called Leopold's attention to problems of Belgian defense
when he had been in office barely a month. His activities, Rumigny
went on, raised a whole host of questions – especially, who is the great
enemy? All this, he noted could be raised by Guizot with Leopold personally since the King of the Belgians had left that very morning (October 5,
1847) for Paris. With this report the ambassador enclosed an anti-
French pamphlet written by an artillery officier (Enens) believed to be
a member of the special commission to study defence problems. The
pamphlet pointed out, among other things, that France was the only
neighboring country that for two centuries had shown itself hostile
to Belgian independence.[3]

Public expression of anti-French sentiment was to be a continuing
problem for Rogier's government. Radicals collected, formed organ-
izations, and aired their views with relative freedom. Brussels as a
hotbed of intellectual radicalism was the price, as Rumigny saw it,
that Belgium paid for being so free. He regarded the price as high in

---

[1] *Ibid.*

[2] There was general agreement on d'Hoffschmidt's affability and conciliatory disposition.
The Austrians also were alerted to the problems facing the new Belgian ministry in its attempt to follow a moderate policy. The government could not make important concessions
to the radicals without losing the moderates and it needed the support of both groups. In
this potential rupture lay opportunity for the Catholics who could become a rallying point
for those seeking order and stability in the face of radical excesses. See Lützow to Metternich,
Aug. 16, 1847, AEV.

[3] Rumigny to Guizot, Oct. 5, 1847, AEF, Belg., XXIX.

terms of the obvious dangers involved. It was especially dangerous because of the status of neutrality in European affairs which Belgium was supposed to maintain. However, with Poles in Brussels celebrating lost dreams, with talks of a democratic organization to hasten emancipation movements in all Europe, with Engels (and Koerner) arriving in exile from France and meeting the acclamations of a hero's welcome, and with Bakunin speaking there against Guizot and Louis Philippe in the guise of language professing true affection for France,[1] all this led naturally to French protests.

From the French point of view the Belgian government itself was implicated. Some anti-French articles in *l'Indépendance* prompted Rumigny to carry his complaints to both Rogier and the King. Leopold agreed with Rumigny and made it clear that he entertained serious doubts that his ministers were acting wisely. Rumigny professed French goodwill for Belgium and indicated that such articles could only cause friction. Rogier also agreed and indicated that he felt *l'Indépendance* should have been more moderate. Rogier at once approached the editor (Sr Terrot) and bluntly told him that if he did not put an end to the obvious hostility to the French government, the cabinet would formally disavow him. Within two days the tone of the paper was modified. D'Hoffschmidt wrote a dispatch to the Prince de Ligne expressing Belgian regret over the ill-will created by the paper. He also showed this to Rumigny and explained the action Rogier had taken.[2]

The Austrians and Prussians also shared in a similar problem of Belgian protection of radicals. A Prussian named Bornstedt had settled in Brussels and wrote in slanderous language about not only the Prussian king but also the Austrian emperor and the new king of Denmark. There were a series of anti-Austrian articles which flowed from his pen and Woyna characterized him as a passionate demagogue who was promoting pure communism. While he was writing a steady stream of revolutionary material and organizing workers' clubs, both the Austrian and Prussian ministers in Brussels lodged strong protests with d'Hoffschmidt. The foreign minister promised that the cabinet would consider the case but Woyna expected little results. As he saw it, the Belgian government was watching all this "without saying any-

---

[1] Rumigny to Guizot, Dec. 1, 1847, Feb. 18, 1848, *ibid.* There were also in Brussels many German workers who had come into the country just prior to the elections and the Austrian ambassador reported vigorous measures taken to prevent communist rioting and other civil disturbances; Woyna to Metternich, May 14, 1847, AEV.

[2] Rumigny to Guizot, Jan. 22, Feb. 1, 1848, AEF, Belg., XXIX.

thing, without doing anything" because it feared an uproar from liberal societies whose support it needed. Legally Woyna believed the government had sufficient latitude to deal with such excesses and could readily expel alien propagandists. The problem was thus not a lack of means but a lack of the courage to face the censures of liberal opinion.[1]

As far as relations with Prussia were concerned, the new ministry in Brussels promptly made sure that its liberal program was explained and understood by the Prussian foreign minister. In foreign affairs Belgium was going to pursue a role of strict impartiality and goodwill based on the treaties assuring Belgian independence and neutrality. Unlike Paris, the change of ministry in Brussels created little interest in Berlin, only one paper, the *Gazette Générale de Prusse*, concerning itself with Belgian affairs. Here, however, the reaction was something of a surprise to Nothomb, Belgium's ambassador to Prussia. This paper had been hostile to every Belgian ministry since 1840 but was now favorable to the cabinet in Brussels. Nothomb read this as a good sign since the paper was a semi-official government organ.[2]

The Leclercq incident occasioned an extensive exchange of letters between d'Hoffschmidt and Nothomb. Nothomb reported (October 8) that the incident had caused a small sensation among some politicians in Berlin. On October 30 he wrote that Baron Canitz' view was that if Belgium wished to reestablish relations with Rome, she should name a new minister and consider the incident closed. D'Hoffschmidt defended the action of the ministry and explained the intricacies of the situation. He maintained that the liberal cabinet had followed common usage scrupulously and explained the British practice of sending agents to other courts. He went on to ask for further information on what the procedure was regarding the sending of Prussian diplomatic envoys to other courts.[3]

Prussian concern in the Leclercq incident however was relatively minor - affairs in Switzerland were much more pressing for them.[4] There were many things disturbing and clouding the international

[1] Woyna to Metternich, Feb. 8, 1848, AEV; and d'Hoffschmidt to Haussy, Feb. 8, 1848, D M, V.

[2] D'Hoffschmidt to Nothomb, Aug. 12, 20, 1847; and Nothomb to d'Hoffschmidt, Aug. 26, 1847, AEB, Pr., VIII.

[3] D'Hoffschmidt to Nothomb, Oct. 1, 6, 8, Nov. 10, 1847; and Nothomb to d'Hoffschmidt, Oct. 8, 9, 15, 16, 30, 1847, *ibid*. To buttress and amplify his statement of the Liberal Government's position, d'Hoffschmidt included with the letter of Oct. 1, 1847, to Nothomb, other correspondence he had had with the Papal Nonce, Mgr. de St. Marsan; d'Hoffschmidt to Nonce, Sept. 17, 28, 1847, and Nonce to d'Hoffschmidt, Sept. 28, 1847.

[4] See, for example, King of Prussia to Victoria, Nov. 25, 1847. LV, II, 161–163.

scene as 1847 ended and 1848 began. D'Hoffschmidt analyzed the
position of Belgium in a letter to Nothomb. The small nation enjoyed
relative tranquility and this he attributed to the fact that actually
Belgium had no really radical or revolutionary party of any size. There
were instead two great opinions in the nation and these were able to
exist side by side within the framework of the constitution. It was a
comforting situation and d'Hoffschmidt was optimistic.[1]

All such questions soon became minor when at 11 A.M. on February
24, 1848, Firmin Rogier, the older brother of Charles, wrote hastily
from the Belgian Embassy in Paris that events were then occurring of
such proportions that "it threatens to become a revolution." [2] It was
indeed a revolution as Louis Philippe abdicated and the Republic was
proclaimed. This French situation was fraught with the most explosive
and frightening possibilities for Belgium and, according to the Austrian
ambassador, the news from Paris was reported in Brussels with a sense
of dread.[3] Rogier's government was untried and distrusted by the king.
The population was overwhelmingly Roman Catholic in religion but
otherwise sharply divided into Walloons and Flemings. The country
was still so new that it was hardly yet a nation and the traditions
present were distinctly not propitious for Belgian unity.

---

[1] D'Hoffschmidt to Nothomb, Feb. 9, 1848, AEB, Pr., IX. Similar letters went to all
members of the Belgian diplomatic corps;; see CNB, I, 1–3.
[2] Firmin Rogier to Charles Rogier, Feb. 24 (11 a.m.), 1848, RP, 126.
[3] Woyna to Metternich, Feb. 26, 1848, AEV.

CHAPTER IV

THE REVOLUTION'S INITIAL IMPACT

The news of revolutionary outbursts in Paris filtered into Brussels in bits and pieces, beginning on the evening of February 24. On the 25th, a variety of reports arrived before both rail and telegraph contact was broken off.[1] The evening of the 25th, the Comte de Hompesch arrived in Brussels with the first news of the proclamation of the Republic. It was common knowledge in the city the next day.[2]

News of the revolution reached London between 4 and 5 P.M. on the 25th. The Belgian ambassador, Van de Weyer, chanced to be in the office of the "Times" when the telegraphic dispatch arrived. He personally carried the word to Prince Albert who in turn broke the news to Queen Victoria. Van de Weyer described her deeply emotional reaction as both touching and noble.[3] A somewhat similar emotional response occurred on the part of Leopold's wife, Louise, Queen of the Belgians and a daughter of Louis Philippe. She wrote to Victoria of her apprehension for the safety of her parents and rhetorically asked how it could be possible that "such events... should be the end of nearly eighteen years of courageous and successful efforts to maintain order, peace, and make France happy..." While questioning how it could be, however, she went on to note philosophically that *"It was the Almighty's will: we must submit."* [4] The King of Prussia also wrote to Victoria professing to see in events "the avenging hand of the King of Kings." He felt that Louis Philippe had given Europe "eighteen years of peace" but that now for some reason "God has permitted events which decisively threaten the peace of Europe." He warned that the fates of all kings were involved and that, in the face of a danger

---

[1] Woyna to Metternich, Feb. 25, 1848, AEV.

[2] J. Dhondt, "La Belgique en 1848," *Actes du Congrès Historique du centenaire de la révolution de 1848* (Paris, 1948), p. 115. See also Hymans, *Frère-Orban*, I, 198; and Discailles, *Rogier*, III, 229–230.

[3] Van de Weyer to Leopold, Feb. 25, 1848, VWP, 116. Greville presents (VI, 20–33) various early accounts of the revioluton in Paris.

[4] Louise to Victoria, Feb. 28, 1848, LV, II, 179–182.

more pressing even than in 1830, the monarchs of Europe must speak in a loud and unified voice to France. Palmerston's presence in the foreign office was, he confessed, a source of comfort and assurance, despite earlier disagreements.[1]

Leopold's first reaction to early reports of trouble in Paris was to suggest to Rogier a careful watch of the frontier, especially near Lille.[2] When the enormity of the change in Paris came home to him, he faced up to the fact that he might be deposed himself. What about his property and his fortune? A large portion of it already was outside the country – he had steadily amassed new lands and this process had occupied much of his efforts [3] – in this respect he resembled Louis Philippe [4] – and he at once started sending shipments of "precious" goods to Claremont in Great Britain.[5]

The king's personal reactions were on the gloomy side and the company of Louise was an equally unsettling influence. The state of his mind on the 26th is clear as we read in his letter to Victoria: "I am very unwell in consequence of the *awful* events at Paris. How will this end? Poor Louise is in a state of despair which is pitiful to behold. What will soon become of us God alone knows; great efforts will be made to revolutionise this country; as there are poor and wicked people in all countries it may succeed." [6]

It should be recalled here that he had often complained about the crown that he wore, especially its weakness.[7] In contemplation of frightful possibilities, he appeared before the cabinet on February 26, 1848,[8] and offered to abdicate.[9] He had spoken in such a vein to Chazal, and to the cabinet he expressed himself with gestures and great emotion. He declared that he had made great sacrifices for the Belgian people but that he was prepared to leave if it would make things easier. The ministers reacted with warm statements of personal loyalty. They

---

[1] King of Prussia to Victoria, Feb. 27, 1848, *ibid.*, 177–179.

[2] Leopold to Rogier, Febr. 25, 1848, RP, 107.

[3] Woyna to Metternich, Feb. 27, 1848, AEV.

[4] Bowring, *Recollections*, pp. 259–260.

[5] Dhondt, "La Belgique," p. 115 note; and Louise to Victoria, Feb. 28, 1848, LV, II, 179–182.

[6] Leopold to Victoria, Feb. 26, 1848, LV, II, 176 (also in Bronne, *Lettres*, p. 212), and Louise to Victoria, Feb. 27, 1848, LV, II, 176–177.

[7] Woyna to Metternich, May 11, 1847, AEV; HP, II, 625; Discailles, *Rogier*, III, 228–229; and also note the reference in the London *Times*, Mar. 1, 1848.

[8] Woyna to Metternich, Feb. 27, 1848, AEV.

[9] In a footnote Dhondt ("La Belgique," pp. 115–116) reviews some of the evidence that Leopold offered to abdicate. Word of his offer became part of a court deposition made in Antwerp in Aug., 1848 (Bertrand, *Démocratie*, I, 276–278). This deposition was based on third hand knowledge. Jottrand learned it from Braas who had it from Lebeau.

were firmly attached to the ideal of a constitutional monarchy and had no desire to see a change in form, despite earlier differences with Leopold.

Evidence of this episode is the letter of Count Woyna to Metternich of March 2, 1848 (AEV). He described Leopold as paralyzed in heart and spirit and weakened by sober foresight. This first bit of weakness on Leopold's part enhanced his prestige with the cabinet and made it easier for the Liberal ministers to turn all their attention to a threatening situation that was soon to grow acute. Leopold shortly recovered his nerve and wrote many letters explaining the policies of Belgium during the crisis to come. The success of Belgium in the next trying months and these positive declarations on his part, obscured from historians the truth of his offer to abdicate and it has lived largely as unconfirmed rumor.[1] This word first was published by Philippe Bourson in the *Journal des Débats* on March 2, 1848, the same day as Woyna's letter mentioned above. Many historians have rejected this abdication account by tracing the rumor to Bourson or, as in Pirenne's case, not even taking it seriously.[2] However, a further corroborating contemporary document which antedates Bourson's account is the report to Palmerston of Mr. Waller at the British Embassy in Brussels. He reported that a member of the diplomatic corps on the best of authority had told him "that King Leopold had laid his own position before his Council, and had enquired of them whether they considered that it might be the means of drawing on this country the anger of the French and of producing a bad effect on its Independence. His Majesty was answered by an instantaneous and unanimous expression of loyalty to his person and attachment to the Belgian constitution as at present established." [3]

In London Prince Albert worried about events in Paris being duplicated in Brussels. Van de Weyer assured him that the populations of

---

[1] Dhondt, "La Belgique," p. 116 note. For positive view that Leopold acted vigorously and did not offer to abdicate, based partially on an assertive letter to Metternich, see Bronne, *Leopold*, p. 225. Woyna specifically discounts this letter by Leopold.

[2] Hymans, *Frère-Orban*, I, 198; Discailles, *Rogier*, III, 235; and Pirenne, *Histoire*, VII, 131.

[3] Waller to Palmerston, Feb. 29, 1848, F.O. 10/137. According to *The Economist* (Mar. 11, 1848), Leopold "offered, it is said, to retire, if he was in the way." Discailles (*Rogier*, III, 235–239) believed Leopold would have yielded before a referendum if the Chamber and Senate had asked that the country be consulted. He notes, however, that there was no such request. At the meeting on the 26th, financial and administrative measures were discussed as well as electoral reform, later introduced by Rogier on the 28th. Rumor of the abdication offer spread quickly, the Russian minister to the Hague showing a letter he received reporting it. The Dutch foreign minister also mentioned it. D'Hoffschmidt wrote Willmar denying that the rumor had any basis in fact. See Willmar to d'Hoffschmidt, Mar. 5, 1848, and d'Hoffschmidt to Willmar, Mar. 8, 1848, CNB, I, 103, 163.

the two capitals were entirely dissimilar politically since in Belgium the initiative for all reform had always come from above and through the government rather than against it.[1] In this context the Austrian ambassador informed Metternich that in Brussels the general opinion was that exactly such a revolution as Paris experienced would have occurred in Brussels had there not been a major change of ministry following the June elections in 1847. Count Woyna concurred in this view and noted that even devoted conservatives in the Catholic Party maintained that the Rogier Ministry was the best guarantee for tranquility and order for Brussels and Belgium.[2] While the ministry would have its hands full worrying about the repercussions from Paris, a further stabilizing factor would be the family connections of Leopold and his vast holdings in personal property. Woyna judged that whatever other motives moved Leopold, the security of his property was tied to conservative principles and this was a motive that could be safely relied on.[3]

A measure of how fluid the situation might have been can be gleaned from two letters from Victor Considerant to Rogier. Considerant had been in Liège giving a series of conferences centered on the phalansterian system of Fourier. At first word of a revolution in Paris, he at once left for Brussels and his letters to Rogier arrived in the early hours of February 26, just before the revolution was common knowledge. In enthusiastic and emotional language he urged Rogier to act at once. He must approach Leopold and the Chamber and convince them to turn Belgium into a republic. It was imperative that Rogier act before the crowds did and Considerant judged that at the most Rogier only had six or eight hours left in which to control events. Thus there could have been no illusions in Rogier's mind about how dedicated radicals would interpret the events in Paris as a call for extensive change elsewhere.[4]

The Liberal government reacted to the events in Paris with a patriotic determination to maintain Belgian order, institutions, and inde-

[1] Van de Weyer to Leopold, Feb. 25, 1848, VWP, 116.

[2] Woyna to Metternich, Feb. 25, 27, 1848, AEV. This was also the judgment currently in the *Times* (Mar. 1, 1848) and later of Bertrand, *Démocratie*, I, 283–284. Rogier's presence at the head of the cabinet instead of de Theux saved the monarchy.

[3] Woyna to Metternich, Feb. 27, 1848, AEV.

[4] Both letters are in Discailles, *Rogier*, III, 232–235. See also Bertrand, *Démocratie*, I, 276, 279–282; and in the *Débat Social*, Mar. 1, 1848, an article, "La Royauté," written probably by Lucien Jottrand who had the confidences of the Comte de Hompesch after he had visited Leopold. This article carried transparent insinuations of governmental modifications. For a tabular presentation of events in Paris and Brussels between Feb. 17–25, see Discailles, *Rogier*, III, 226–230.

pendence. Leopold moved into Brussels at the cabinet's request, a wise move in terms of safety and also urban morale. There was confidence in both the army and the civic guard as plans were made to move firmly against any domestic insurrection. Immediate trouble was expected only from a handful of foreign democrats in some of the clubs in Brussels. Thirty of these were promptly arrested, some found with poignards and large sums of money. A number disappeared, among them the German Bornstedt who was believed to have fled to Paris. His arrest had been specifically decreed and in concert with the Prussian minister, Count Seckendorff, measures were taken to prevent his return which was expected in a few days. Exactly the kind of vigor Count Woyna had vainly called for earlier against the radicals was now the policy of the government. Chazal exuded confidence in his army and Rogier was determined to be both firm and moderate. While ready to repress instantly any violation of the law, he was equally resolved not to exceed the law. Woyna indeed felt that Leopold had been a weak example in offering to abdicate and that he must be more forceful. In fact, his problem now was to associate himself somehow with the vigor and energy displayed by the government and to be more a part of the nation's leadership. The move from Laeken into the city was a good first step.[1]

The danger was not regarded as centering so much on domestic insurrection as on a French invasion and Woyna estimated that the Belgian government could probably maintain control in every other contingency. To meet armed aggression the Belgian ministry would need to feel that substantial aid was at once forthcoming. Thus Woyna saw it as essential that Prussian troops be concentrated along Belgium's eastern frontier.[2]

The alternative was a specific guarantee from Britain and in London Van de Weyer was reminding Palmerston and others of Belgium's grave position. He urged concrete plans – such as some of the British fleet in the Escaut – for meeting the "ambitious projects of the Revolutionary government." He gave assurances that his country was

---

[1] Woyna to Metternich, Feb. 27, Mar. 2, 1848, AEV; Haussy to d'Hoffschmidt, Mar. 2, 1848, DM, V; Bertrand, *Démocratie*, I, 300–306, 311–312; Waller to Palmerston, Feb. 29, 1848, and Walden to Palmerston, Mar. 4, 1848, F.O. 10/137. Bornstedt was killed April 28, 1848, in a column of German workers, defeated and dispersed between Schopfheim and Dossenbach near the Swiss frontier. See M.A. Lefebvre to Lamartine, Apr. 29, 1848, DD,I, 1088.

[2] Woyna to Metternich, Feb. 27, 1848, AEV. For convincing indications of a deliberate attack on Belgium, see [Houry] to d'Hoffschmidt, Mar. 1, 1848, CNB, I, 41. Seven French regiments were reported being moved to the Franco-Belgian frontier.

ready to fight "the natural enemies of its independence." As he put it, "a republican France was an aggressive and conquering France." Palmerston replied that the situation was truly grave – so grave that cabinet action only could approve such a use of British ships. He went on to inquire of the condition of Belgium's fortresses.[1] D'Hoffschmidt's reaction to Van de Weyer's request for the fleet was to admonish him that such a request was premature and perhaps dangerous. He reminded his ambassador that such a request could cause all sort of French resentment. So far the Provisional Government was peaceful regarding Belgium and no French army corps appeared ready to invade Belgium. He further reminded Van de Weyer of Belgium's neutrality and ordered him neither to mention his request again to Palmerston nor to do anything like it again without specific orders.[2] Van de Weyer replied that at the time he approached Palmerston, news of an immediate invasion of Belgium had arrived in London and the British cabinet itself had believed it was well-founded. The need was urgent to find out what measures Britain would take in Belgium's defence and the sending of a fleet was only one possibility. His talks with Palmerston had not been official and he had allowed the whole matter to drop.[3] Though Van de Weyer was rebuffed for his efforts, it was natural that the Belgians should turn to Britain for reassurance should the crisis get out of hand.

At the same time Leopold personally wrote to Metternich and to the Archduke John, arguing that mutual safety required that the four powers (Austria, France, Prussia, Britain) renew the guarantes of the Conference of London. Such a union was absolutely essential to prevent, as Leopold put it, the complete dissolution of society in Europe. Austria especially could not afford to contemplate the spread of propaganda promoting disorder in hereditary states. He saw Austria as the power that could best act as a mediator with Metternich having another opportunity to prove and enhance his stature as a great statesman. He was emphatic that Great Britain truly favored friendly relations with the Austrian court and he pointedly noted that Austria would suffer from a policy of isolation.[4]

While these letters were probably en route, Metternich was penning his analysis of the situation, especially regarding the British. He ap-

---

[1] Van de Weyer to Leopold, Feb. 27, 1848, VWP, 116 (also in CNB, I, 6–8).
[2] D'Hoffschmidt to Van de Weyer, Feb. 29, 1848, CNB, I, 132–134.
[3] Van de Weyer to d'Hoffschmidt, Mar. 3, 1848, *ibid.*, 68–69.
[4] Leopold to Metternich, Feb. 28, 1848, and Leopold to Archduke John, near the end of Feb., 1848 (no date, no signature), drafts, AEV. Leopold warned that Austria's status as a Russian ally would come to resemble that of the Sultan.

proved of what he had heard from Woyna of Belgium's early posture of firmness after the fall of Louis Philippe. While there might be a few partisans in Belgium desiring a union with France, Metternich wrote that he was sure "the people ought not to wish" such a thing. Rather than Austria holding the power of decision and initiative as Leopold suggested, Metternich saw everything now turning on Britain – and the hopes were meager. The British cabinet was directly responsible for the current difficult situation in Italy. Its view that a struggle was going on between Italian liberalisn and Austrian obscurantism was naive. The British had opened the flood-gates to radicalism in Italy by following policies based on ignorance and arrogance. None the less, Austria could be counted on to do its duty! What this duty implied the Prince failed to indicate but by implication he approved of Belgian resistance to French aggression should it occur and he also specifically welcomed the idea of close cooperation between the Belgians and Prussians.[1]

Thus there appeared little chance of British-Austrian cooperation but at least both powers wished Belgium well and the possibility of Prussian support was clearly a reasonable hope. In addition, through regular diplomatic channels the Belgian ministry received a completely spontaneous assurance from the Dutch government that it would support Belgian independence and neutrality. The past relations of the two states made this something of a surprise and it was welcomed with enthusiasm and satisfaction.[2]

The Belgian Chamber of Deputies and Senate dramatized the support enjoyed by the ministry after the revolution in Paris. Sitting together, they unanimously approved two bills calculated to meet the exigencies of the moment. One would facilitate the entry of foreign capital into the nation and the other promoted uniformity in the franchise requirements. This happy unanimity Woyna read as a true reflection of Belgian society where he saw the nobility ready to make monetary sacrifices in good faith, industrialists coping with employment needs, businessmen striving to uphold public credit, priests preaching loyalty and support for the government they had recently opposed, and the bourgeoisie joining the civic guard in order to keep order in the streets against the threat of foreign agitators. The urban populations of Belgium were quiet, however, and the soldier was ready to obey any orders his officers would give. There was no popular

[1] Metternich to Leopold, Mar. 4, 1848, AEV.
[2] Woyna to Metternich, Mar. 3, 1848, AEV.

following for alien ideas, l'homme en blouse talked in a language of loyalty and opposition to any French agitators. There was a mood of stability and common-sense rather than emotional volatility.[1]

This atmosphere was noted by the new French ambassador, Sérurier. He observed to Lamartine that Belgium already had the liberties for which the French had just gone to arms. A great deal of attention in Brussels was given to the financial situation with an awareness of possible crisis at any moment. Nonetheless, all important groups were reacting in the best interests of the nation; even Leopold was being a proper constitutional monarch, seeing his royalty more as a philosopher than a prince. Sérurier reported his own efforts to reduce the activities and enthusiasm of a number of French propagandists. There was no reason, he felt, for the French government to fear any trouble or change occurring in Belgium.[2] This conclusion was also d'Hoffschmidt's who sent word to Leopold that, despite activities of some republicans, there were no grounds to fear a French invasion and no need to continue with efforts to involve the powers signatory to the treaties of 1839.[3] The confused atmosphere of the first days after February 24 had passed and with it the period of greatest danger.

* * *

On February 24, 1848, Louis Philippe diligently wrote out his abdication while his son, the Duke of Montpensier, urged him to make it quick.[4] As he hastily left Paris, it was as though he moved out of contact with most of the world; and, as might be expected, rumor filled the gap. As late as March 1, Victoria did not know whether Louis Philippe and his family were in France or Britain. The word that they were really with Leopold at Laeken was branded as untrue and Palmerston was advised that such a report should be denied.[5] Where the illustrious fugitives were became an intriguing temporary mystery.[6]

---

[1] Woyna to Metternich, Mar. 5, 1848, AEV. The British ambassador also sent home a similar analysis; Walden to Palmerston, Mar. 4, 1848, F.O. 10/137. For additional important reform measures, see Bertrand, Démocratie, I, 298–299.

[2] Sérurier to Lamartine, Mar. 17, 1848, AEF, Belg., XXX.

[3] To Leopold (probably from d'Hoffschmidt and in early March, copy, undated and unsigned, maybe before Mar. 8), DM, V.

[4] Charles George Barrington, "Recollections of Lord Palmerston," History Today, XI, 3 (Mar. 1961), 182–190. Louis Philippe: "Il faut un peu de temps même pour abdiquer."

[5] Victoria to Leopold, Mar. 1, 1848, LV, II, 183; and Waller to Palmerston, Feb. 26, 1848, F.O. 10/137. On Mar. 1, the Times rumored Louis Philippe as in Brussels; on Mar. 4, the Times reported him to have dropped out of sight completely.

[6] Featherstonhaugh (British consul at Havre) to Palmerston, Mar. 3, 1848, LV, II, 184–188, a detailed account of the deposed royalty leaving France. For their trip from Paris, see Thureau-Dangin, Monarchie, VII, 522–523.

There is no question that British authorities were uncertain of Louis Philippe's destination. Hence the Admiralty dispatched a number of steamships to various French ports, each ordered to be at the disposition of the deposed royalty.[1] In Brussels the rumor by the morning of February 26 was that Louis Philippe was headed towards the Chateau d'Eu and was on his way to Britain.[2] The King of the Belgians was implicated in much of the uncertainty. One of Leopold's military household said the king had received from Brighton a letter written in the personal hand of Louis Philippe. However, two days later, on March 1, Leopold said he had no news yet on Louis Philippe's place of retirement. The Austrian ambassador speculated that since British journals were announcing positively that he was not in Britain, perhaps somebody wanted to suggest that Louis Philippe was somewhere in Belgium.[3] Woyna connected the mystery with Van Praet's trip to Paris which suggested a contact with the deposed monarch.[4] Van Praet had left for Paris by rail on the evening of February 25. His biographer, Carlo Bronne, sketches briefly the trip to Paris but makes no suggestion that it was anything more than a matter of getting information on current conditions in that troubled city.[5] Though it was apparent that neither the king nor members of the cabinet could speak with authority on the whereabouts of Louis Philippe, the Queen of the Belgians was extremely nervous and upset by the course of events, but suddenly (about March 1) became calm and showed no signs of agitation.[6] Count Woyna speculated that Louis Philippe was reticent about going to Britain and was hiding in Belgium while trying to decide what to do. Possibly he was still amazed that the throne which he had believed durable and solidly based could have been overthrown so swiftly.[7] It was indeed the season for second thoughts and among those believing that the throne need not have fallen were Madame de Lieven and Queen Victoria.[8] By March 3, it was acknowledged publicly that the deposed monarchs were in Great Britain and the journals now

---

[1] Van de Weyer to Leopold, Feb. 28, 1848, VWP, 116.

[2] Woyna to Metternich, Feb. 26, 1848, AEV. The Château d'Eu was the ex-king's objective until he learned that the regency had not been accepted. See Thureau-Dangin, *Monarchie*, VII, 522.

[3] Woyna to Metternich, Mar. 2, 3, 1848, AEV.

[4] Woyna to Metternich, Mar. 3, 1848, AEV.

[5] Bronne, *Jules Van Praet*, p. 36. For lack of communication, see Waller to Palmerston, Feb. 25, 1848, F.O. 10/137.

[6] Woyna to Metternich, Mar. 3, 1848, AEV.

[7] Woyna to Metternich, *Ibid.*

[8] Greville, *Memoirs*, VI, 40 (Mar. 16, 1848); Victoria to Leopold, Mar. 11, 1848; and Victoria to Melbourne, Mar. 15, 1848, LV, II, 194–195.

published all sorts of detailed information on Louis Philippe's fall from power.[1]

Although Victoria was openly critical of the general policies which had led to Louis Philippe's downfall, her heart was touched when she actually saw the regal refugees. She referred to them, in a letter to Leopold, as "our poor French relations." On March 6 they looked to her like "humbled poor people." [2] The recent king (now the Count of Neuilly) spoke of "cette révolution de Janissaires" and Van de Weyer reported the meeting as "penible et touchante." [3] John Russell had suggested to the queen another context in which whole the episode could be viewed, It was, he wrote, perhaps "no irremediable calamity if a Prince of great powers of mind and warm domestic affection is permitted by Providence to end his days in peace and tranquility." [4]

Just where in Britain the French king would reside "to end his days in peace and tranquility" was another problem. As the royal family arrived in London, Van de Weyer arranged housing at Claremont for these "augustes infortunes" and offered to do all that he could without compromising his position as the Belgian ambassador. His efforts to acquire funds for them were refused by the Duke of Nemours though Louis Philippe needed money. He had escaped with only £ 10,000 sterling and some diamonds. In Belgium Leopold was holding other diamonds for the ex-king. This was the extent of his wealth and Greville soberly reported that "beggary is actually staring them in the face." A certain amount of ill-will had attended Louis Philippe's coming to Britain but this was dissipated when it was learned that he no longer possessed a vast fortune. Claremont then was owned by Leopold. Palmerston questioned the propriety of his living there on a permanent basis and others talked of it as well. However, when the Duke of Wellington visited Louis, he told him that Claremont was perfectly appropriate. Word of the old duke's opinion circulated along with the news of the ex-king's lack of funds and public criticism lessened on this score as well. Meanwhile Leopold wrote that he could reside at Claremont as long as he liked. The earlier criticism had irked Louis Philippe who was already in a bad mood. To visitors he described his fall and flight as a very personal thing and his language carried no hint of patriotism or of feeling

---

[1] Woyna to Metternich, Mar. 3, 7, 1848, AEV. On Mar. 6, 1848, the *Times* reported that in Brussels on Mar. 4, the impression was that Louis Philippe had gone to Germany.
[2] Victoria to Leopold, Mar. 1, 7, 1848, LV, II, 183–184, 193.
[3] Van de Weyer to Leopold, Mar. 7, 1848, VWP, 116.
[4] John Russell to Victoria, Mar. 3, 1848, LV, II, 191.

for his country. He gave the impression of being a most uncomfortable pauper.[1]

Despite having lost his throne, Louis Philippe continued, with Guizot's assistance, to pursue a policy in Spanish affairs as though he were still in power. Unfortunately this was an anti-British policy and brought outspoken criticism from Palmerston. Victoria found it al heart-rending and from spells of tears counseled forgetting about the whole episode of the Spanish marriages.[2]

---

[1] Van de Weyer to Leopold, Feb. 28, Mar. 3, 8, 11, 18, 1848, VWP, 116; Greville, *Memoirs*, VI, 36–38 (Mar. 12, 20, 1848); and Bronne, *Leopold*, p. 226. A number of Louis Philippe's family stayed at East Sheen, at a suburban villa of Mr. Bates, father-in-law of Van de Weyer (*Times*, Mar. 2, 1848). Louis Philippe's account of his fall varied from Guizot's description.
[2] Van de Weyer to Leopold, Mar. 7, 10, 11, 1848, VWP, 116; Greville, *Memoirs*, VI, 69–70 (June 1, 1848); and *The Economist*, Mar. 18, 1848.

CHAPTER V

EARLY RELATIONS WITH THE PROVISIONAL GOVERNMENT

After the flight of Louis Philippe there was an uneasy interim in Franco-Belgian relations before the new Provisional Government was in full diplomatic contact with Brussels. As late as the morning of February 29, d'Hoffschmidt had had no official word from the Provisional Government. Neither had he received any French newspapers nor any dispatch from the Prince de Ligne. On the 28th, d'Hoffschmidt instructed the Prince to remain at Paris and to adopt, until the situation was clear, the same attitude as his colleagues from other constitutional states.[1]

In Brussels the French embassy had ceased communication with the Belgian ministry. During this anxious interlude, the Belgians increased the garrisons at Mons, Charleroi, and Philippeville, as part of a general strengthening of the frontier facing France. D'Hoffschmidt sent word to Palmerston that the Belgians really had no immediate apprehension of attack from France. Their precautions, however, belied such a remark; and the message carried a reminder that in the face of an organized invasion, Belgium would call for aid from those powers which had guaranteed Belgian neutrality.[2] D'Hoffschmidt also wrote to Van de Weyer, asking his opinion regarding an immediate Belgian recognition of the Provisional Government. He particularly wanted a report on the reactions of the major powers, especially Britain, to such an action, which, he indicated had almost been decided.[3]

In London the ambassadors of the Northern Powers reacted to what they judged was a period of crisis and emergency. In a Secret Memo of February 27, 1848, edited by Brunnow and sent to Palmerston,

---

[1] D'Hoffschmidt to Ligne, Feb. 28, 1848, CNB, I, 14.

[2] Waller to Palmerston, Feb. 29, 1848, F.O. 10/137.

[3] D'Hoffschmidt to Van de Weyer, Mar. 2, 1848, CNB, I, 51. D'Hoffschmidt also asked Willmar's opinion which was as follows: Belgian neutrality demanded prompt and unofficial relations with the Provisional Government and that Belgium stay neutral in case of a conflict between France and other powers. If her relations were official, Belgium would be blamed. See Willmar to d'Hoffschmidt, Mar. 7, 1848, ibid., 140–142.

they tried to secure British support or adhesion to the principles of
1815. Brunnow was openly advocating war. Dietrichstein believed
hostilities were inevitable; and, while Austria would not *start* action
against France, direct provocation would probably come from Italy.
According to the memo, the principles of 1815 in the context of 1848
prompted the conclusion that the monarchic principle must be maintained for the repose of Europe, territories generally should be defined
as of 1815 and if France were to cause trouble, the allies must be
resolved to concert on effective measures. The ambassadors of the
Northern Powers agreed to these general statements and sent copies
of the memo to their home governments as well as to Palmerston. Van
de Weyer sent a copy to Nothomb. Palmerston tended not to act so
precipitantly and urged Prussia not to allow a Russian army to pass
through Germany.[1] Van de Weyer had already reminded Palmerston
of Belgium's precarious position and of the guarantees made earlier
to the new state.[2] On the 28th, Van de Weyer wrote that while the
news from Brussels was good, in Britain the mood seemed to favor
peace at any price.[3] The next day Palmerston informed Van de Weyer
that Normanby had written saying that the new French government
was resolved to maintain peace and had no wish to annex Belgium.
This information was confidential and he cautioned that its premature
publication might weaken the influence of Lamartine.[4]

The situation in Paris was precarious as business came to a standstill
and the government operated in the shadows of growing unemployment
and the fear of mob violence.[5] D'Hoffschmidt read a report that there
was irritation in Paris that the Belgians had not yet revolted; therefore
agents had been sent there and to the Rhenish provinces since Belgium
was indispensable to France and the Rhine would be retaken as soon
as possible.[6] Yet Lamartine was a sign of hope. Woyna noted that
despite "transports of vehemence" Lamartine was born a gentlemen
with a poetic temperament and in little signs of politeness and urbanity

---

[1] Van de Weyer to d'Hoffschmidt, Mar. 3, 1848, *ibid.*, 70–73.

[2] Van de Weyer to Leopold, Feb. 27, 1848, VWP, 116. On the same date Rogier questioned
Britain's embassy about British gunboats at the mouth of the Scheldt, information he had
received from Chazal. Waller expressed ignorance and disbelief; Waller to Palmerston, Feb.
27, 1848, F.O. 10/137. Note (ch. IV) that Van de Weyer on this same day had requested such
an appearance but was put off by Palmerston on the plea that such a serious action would
require cabinet action.

[3] Van de Weyer to d'Hoffschmidt, Feb. 28, 1848, CNB, I, 18.

[4] Van de Weyer to Leopold, Feb. 29, 1848, VWP, 116.

[5] Martin, *Consort*, II, 24.

[6] [Houry] to d'Hoffschmidt, Mar. 1, 1848, CNB, I, 41.

one could see that he had not entirely forgotten or escaped his heritage[1] *Slightly* reassuring also was a report that General Bedeau had clearly affirmed that the Provisional Government had no designs on its neighbors. Harangues to the army were needed to buoy its morale. The sending of regiments to the Belgian frontier was only to appease and satisfy the army and at the same time to observe the Powers of the North.[2]

In Paris the heads of the various missions were caught suddenly in a precarious situation. Had the fall of Louis Philippe automatically ended their diplomatic accreditation? Should they request their passports or wait to see if they were given to them? The doyen of the corps, Austria's Count Apponyi, advised waiting for instructions from home.[3]

The Prince de Ligne at once sized up the situation as being particularly unfortunate for Belgium in two respects: she shared a boundary with France; and Leopold, as a relative of Louis Philippe, would naturally be an object of ill-will from the Provisional Government. Believing the moment required initiative, he visited Lamartine, privately and not as an ambassador, and declared that though he had not yet received instructions from Brussels, he was sure Leopold's main interests were centered in the Belgian people and that he could be depended upon to seek the best possible relations with France, despite his family connection with the House of Orleans. Lamartine seemed to accept these comments at their face value and the prince reported amiable, though unofficial, relations.[4]

On the 27th, Lamartine informed the Prince de Ligne and other ambassadors in Paris that he was the new foreign minister and that France favored the independence of nations and world peace.[5] His

---

[1] Woyna to Metternich, Mar. 9, 1848, AEV.

[2] C. B. Houry to d'Hoffschmidt, Mar. 5, 1848, I, 121–122.

[3] Prince de Ligne, *Souvenirs*, p. 66; and Ligne to d'Hoffschmidt, Feb. 25, 1848, CNB, I, 4–5.

[4] Ligne, *Souvenirs*, pp. 66–67. The Prince reported his actions to d'Hoffschmidt who approved, as did Leopold and the rest of the cabinet. See d'Hoffschmidt to Ligne, Mar. 1, 1848, CNB, I, 37.

[5] Lamartine to diplomatic corps at Paris, Feb.27, 1848, DD, I, 1. Two days later Lamartine circularized French diplomatic agents (*ibid*). that shortly he would send them an extensive statement of policy. This was sent out on Mar. 2, 1848 (*ibid.*, 7–11) and was a moderately worded amplification of the idea that the Republic did not mean war automatically and in fact it desired peace with all other powers. It did make the points though that France did not admit the rights of 1815 but rather the facts of 1815 as a basis for modification. This disturbed Palmerston and also Bunsen, Prussian Minister in London. See Van de Weyer to d'Hoffschmidt, Mar. 5, 1858, CNB, I, 100–102. Ligne called the circular merely a matter of giving satisfaction to public opinion in France. Ligne to d'Hoffschmidt, Mar. 9, 1848, *ibid.*, 171–173. In *The Economist*. Mar, 4, 1848, the reaction was very favorable.

language was regarded by d'Hoffschmidt as moderate and reassuring and he hastily sent a copy of the statement to an anxious Nothomb in Berlin. D'Hoffschmidt instructed the prince to respond politely to Lamartine's message of the 27th but neither to seek out nor to avoid the French minister. He might talk with Lamartine unofficially, but anything of an official character was to be reported to Brussels.Meantime he was to keep in touch with his colleagues, particularly regarding their actions on recognition and was to send d'Hoffschmidt his own opinions regarding recognition.[1]

Although the Prussian position could be predicted as in accord with Austria's, still its attitude would not be positively known for a few days; and, in the meantime, in Berlin, there was an intense anxiety for the security of Belgium. Nothomb's colleagues were as anxious for news as he and they checked with him for whatever information he might receive. As he wrote it, they feared that the revolution in France might signal the formation of a republic in Belgium. This would mean the union of Belgium and France; this would mean a general war; and, finally, a general war meant the extermination of Belgium. The copy of Lamartine's letter was thus a particularly important communication, as also was news of unanimity in Belgium on the forced loan and the nation's general appearance of solidarity.[2] Nothomb's views on the prospects of a republic being proclaimed in Belgium were clear: it simply was not going to happen. Further he felt that Palmerston should emphatically oppose discussions in Parliament positing such an event by openly declaring that it would mean war.[3]

On February 29, the Prince de Ligne wrote to d'Hoffschmidt his opinion of what Belgium should do: recognize the Provisional Government at once; and, at the same time take all precautions for defence. Tell the French that they must respect their neighbors; and though the Belgians respect the revolution, they would fight to defend their sovereignty. At the same time the Provisional Government must not be irritated; pretexts for invasion must be avoided. Early recognition was probably the only means of forestalling an immediate invasion of

---

[1] D'Hoffschmidt to Ligne, Mar. 1, 1848, CNB, I, 39–40. Ligne's opinion written on the 29th had not yet reached d'Hoffschmidt. See note 4, p. 39 and material it supports.

[2] Nothomb to d'Hoffschmidt, Feb. 29, Mar. 1, 1848, and d'Hoffschmidt to Nothomb, Mar. 1, 1848, AEB, Pr., IX. See also d'Hoffschmidt to Nothomb, Feb. 28, 1848, *ibid.* (also in CNB, I, 15–17) where d'Hoffschmidt explains Belgian determination not to become involved in internal affairs of others and also inquires of Prussia's views of the new French government and what instructions it is sending its agent there.

[3] D'Hoffschmidt to Van de Weyer, Mar. 9, 1848, and d'Hoffschmidt to Nothomb, Mar. 9, 1848, CNB, I, 169–170, 173.

Belgium, and, recognizing the likelihood of the latter, Belgium should form an alliance with Britain and with Holland. He ended by asking for instructions, adding that he believed Lamartine was anxious to learn of Belgium's attitude.[1]

It was d'Hoffschmidt's view, written to Ligne on March 1, that relations could only be informal (officieuse) and not official, and that it was best to follow Great Britain's lead. Belgium's relations with a *provisional* government clearly could not be the same as those with a definitive government. Thus the best course now was for the Prince de Ligne's accreditation to be from the minister of foreign affairs and not from the king. By this middle course Belgium might have good relations with republican France while not alienating other European powers.[2] Ligne observed a bit more boldly that Belgium had no need to demand French recognition of its own independence and neutrality. There was no need for mutual reciprocity on the question since it was the French Republic which was new and not the Belgian state. Recognition for the Provisional Republic could thus be made subordinate to a promise that there would be no attack.[3]

Replying to Ligne's opinion of the 29th, d'Hoffschmidt on March 2, instructed the Prince to tell Lamartine of Belgium's desire that traditional good relations with France continue. If Lamartine were to ask if that implied a positive Belgian decision to recognize the Provisional Government, Ligne was to say 'Yes' providing the French recognized Belgian independence and neutrality as stipulated in treaties.[4]

After sending the reassuring word to Nothomb, d'Hoffschmidt instructed the Prince de Ligne to emphasize to the new French government that recent military activity in Belgium was not motivated by any hostility towards France. Belgium only wanted peace and its neutrality maintained. Since her land was so exposed, the nation must be ready to defend itself and in a general conflagration, she could be more readily invaded by armies "from the North" ("du Nord" – a masterful play on words?) than from France, a true neighbor who had aided them in their political emancipation and who was now Belgium's best defense.[5] In addition, d'Hoffschmidt cautioned Ligne against definitely committing Belgium. There was a rumor ("on dit") in

[1] Ligne to d'Hoffschmidt, Feb. 29, 1848, *ibid.*, 26–29, with a copy in Woyna to Metternich, Mar. 5, 1848, AEV.

[2] D'Hoffschmidt to Ligne, Mar. 1, 1848, CNB, I, 37–39.

[3] Ligne to d'Hoffschmidt, Mar. 3, 1848, *ibid.*, I, 63–64.

[4] D'Hoffschmidt to Ligne, Mar. 2, 1848, *ibid.*, I, 53.

[5] D'Hoffschmidt to Ligne, Mar. 4, 1848, IND, I; this also in CNB, I, 92–94.

Brussels that the Provisional Government might send the Duke de Bassano to Brussels. Bassano had lived in Belgium earlier and d'Hoffschmidt regarded him as a good choice. However, he now had the grade of minister plenipotentiary and this raised the question of whether he really would come to Belgium at a lower rank. Ligne was to seek him out in Paris and to press on him the advantages of an unofficial mission with the letters of a simple chargé.[1]

D'Hoffschmidt then informed the Belgian legations at London, Vienna, The Hague, Berlin, and Frankfort that despite Lamartine's desire for peace and promise to respect Belgian independence, in fact Belgium was menaced by revolutionary propaganda at the moment and at all costs must stay on peaceful terms with the French government. In these circumstances Belgium simply could not wait for the convening of the National Assembly to grant recognition. The various ambassadors were to explain these motives to their respective governments.[2]

On March 2, Ligne wrote to d'Hoffschmidt that the Provisional Government was surprised that a republic had not yet been proclaimed in Belgium; and consequently some enrollments, mostly French, had already appeared for a Belgian Legion. The fixed idea of the Rhine as a natural boundary meant that Belgium must adopt a militant defensive attitude; and Ligne's opinion was that if Belgium were close to Britain and Prussia, she might escape invasion. Great Britain would surely not allow Antwerp to become a French port. He had seen Normanby the day before and learned that the British ambassador was to communicate unofficially with the Provisional Government.[3] Lamartine was pleased at the sign of friendly relations between France and Britain but regretted the lack of full recognition which the British implied could not be granted before French elections. The instructions sent to Ligne placed Belgian representation on the same basis.[4]

Lamartine had the problem that not all states were reacting in the same fashion in the matter of recognition. While many were deciding to steer a middle course by means of unofficial relations, the King of

---

[1] See two letters of Mar. 4, 1848, d'Hoffschmidt to Ligne, CNB, I, 94–95, 96–97. D'Hoffschmidt felt Bassano would be an excellent choice as a definitive appointment later. On a provisional basis Leopold believed that M. de la Fressange, the French secretary at the embassy, would be acceptable. He needed neither letters to the King nor full powers for the moment. See d'Hoffschmidt to Ligne, Mar. 7, 1848, *ibid.*, 147–148.

[2] D'Hoffschmidt circular to the legations, Mar. 4, 1848, *ibid.*, 89–92.

[3] Ligne to d'Hoffschmidt, Mar. 2, 1848, *ibid.*, 54–56.

[4] Van de Weyer to d'Hoffschmidt, 2 letters on Mar. 4, 1848, and d'Hoffschmidt to Ligne, Mar. 4, 1848, *ibid.*, 78–80, 97–98.

Bavaria had recognized the French Republic and agreed to a French spokesman in Munich. By March 10, Lamartine had decided that he would send official agents only to those courts who wanted them, until the republic was definitely established. Thus he agreed to a representative in Brussels without letters to the king. He also gave assurances that the new French appointee would receive antipropagandist instructions. The next day G. Sérurier, son of the predecessor of Rumigny, called on Ligne and informed him that he was charged with unofficial relations in Brussels. Ligne regarded Sérurier's antipropagandist instructions as a triumph for his own (Ligne's) efforts and as an act of loyalty towards Belgium on the part of Lamartine.[1]

In the Chamber of Deputies on March 1, the Liberal government was subjected to a careful questioning. Castiau, an ultra-liberal who had a number of queries, called the upheaval in Paris perhaps the greatest event in modern times, a sign of the inevitability that the principles of liberty and equality would tour the world. To this rhetoric a more restrained liberal, Delfosse, drew loud applause by noting that such French principles could make their tour without having to go through Belgium since she was already blessed with liberty and equality. D'Hoffschmidt openly described the tenuous contact with the new government, limited really to Lamartine's first announcement to the Prince de Ligne and other ambassadors. Replying to questions regarding some minor arrests, the minister of justice, Haussy, claimed that the government was not out to take ridiculous measures and Charles Rogier firmly insisted that order must be preserved, that Belgian hospitality, while open to everyone, was not a license for disorder. The government was strong and the nation was secure. A careful watch was being kept, Rogier maintained, and so far there was no reason to restrict the free expression of opinions. Delfosse congratulated the government on its patriotism and resolution and declared

---

[1] Lamartine to Ligne, Mar. 5, 1848, Ligne to d'Hoffschmidt, Mar. 6, 1848, and d'Hoffschmidt to Ligne, Mar. 7, 1848, CNB, I, 136–139, 147–148. In an unofficial capacity and without a court presentation, M. Cottu, former French attaché at London, was the new French spokesman in Britain succeeding de Jarnac. See Van de Weyer to d'Hoffschmidt, Mar. 9, 1848, ibid., 168. See also Ligne to d'Hoffschmidt, Mar. 10, 11, 1848, ibid., 177–179, 185–187. The meeting on the 10th was erroneously reported as official rather than unofficial in the Journal des Débats. The next day (Mar. 11) Ligne wrote of tendencies in Paris to report "officieux" as official and that it was hard to tell whether this was the fault of the government or merely of the journals. He noted an attack on Belgium in the National. D'Hoffschmidt noted the errors, said they would be publicly corrected in reports in Brussels but that a fuss should not be made over them. In a note to the Belgian diplomatic corps he advised prudence in the face of the hostility of the National, Courrier Française, and others. See Ligne to d'Hoffschmidt, Mar. 11, 1848, d'Hoffschmidt to Ligne, Mar. 12, 1848, and d'Hoffschmidt to Belg. dipl. corps, Mar. 13, 1848, ibid., 189–190, 194–195, 198–199.

that in such circumstances, petty squabbles should be put aside in the interest of national well-being. *L'Indépendance* stressed also the need for solidarity – in union and order the Belgian people would demonstrate their support for their institutions.[1] While liberal at home, Belgium was to have a conservative foreign policy. Her diplomacy would recognize the absolute freedom of peoples to decide for themselves their own governments without intervention by outsiders and at the same time support the stipulated rights in existing treaties.[2]

Diplomatic relations with the Provisional Government created a problem for all the powers of Europe, and especially for Belgium. It was ironic that in the matter of exchanging ambassadors and taking the lead in *de facto* recognition of the new regime, it fell to Belgium's lot to be among the first. In Count Woyna's opinion, if a new French ambassador were sent to Brussels, a failure to receive him by the Belgians would be tantamount to declaring war on the republican government. This kind of courageous response by the Belgian government could only be expected if large numbers of Prussian troops were held in readiness between Cologne and Aix-la-Chapelle, in case such a refusal led to an immediate French invasion.[3] Woyna's estimate was that a different course of events would ensue. On March 5, he wrote that Belgium knew its role as a small power and realized that she was not expected to take any initiative in major international questions. Her neutrality depended on the preservation of peace and the Belgians were sensible enough to recognize that they needed the cooperation of the major powers. Past Belgian diplomacy had generally followed the views of the British. However, in the current situation it was reasonable that the Belgian government would want normal relations established with the French government as soon as possible. This, of course, ran counter to British views; and Woyna concluded that Belgium would have to proceed very carefully, since its treaties implied at the very least, consultation with the powers guaranteeing its position.[4]

Meantime, some of Woyna's colleagues in the diplomatic corps were

---

[1] H.P., II, 662–663, 656, 677; Waller to Palmerston, Mar. 1, 1848, F.O. 10/137; Bertrand, *Démocratie*, I, 292–293; and Discailles, *Rogier*, III, 240–241. The *Gazette de Prusse*, Mar. 6, 1848, reproduced the Belgian discussions with favorable commentary, especially for Delfosse's remarks. See Nothomb to d'Hoffschmidt, Mar. 6, 1848, CNB, I, 130.

[2] Van de Weyer in Bemmel, *Patria*, II, 343–344.

[3] Woyna to Metternich, Feb. 27, 1848, AEV.

[4] Woyna to Metternich, Mar. 5, 1848, *ibid*. In Paris Normanby had implied British recognition if the European balance of power were left undisturbed. Lamartine indicated that the treaties of 1815 no longer existed but that France recognized the existing territorial limits of the countries of Europe. See *The Economist*, Mar. 4, 11, 1858.

convinced that the Belgian cabinet intended to recognize the Provisional Government as the *de facto* government and that this pure and simple act of recognition would place the major European powers in an awkward position. Woyna, however, disagreed, his views being based on talks he had had with Frère-Orban, Rogier, and d'Hoffschmidt. To remove the chance of doubt, he asked d'Hoffschmidt point-blank whether the Belgian government intended to recognize the Provisional Government formally. He accompanied the question with a statement of the obvious, that Belgium, after all, was not the only power concerned. D'Hoffschmidt replied that Belgium's political dependence was not a condition of its neutrality. Woyna protested that he had not meant to imply this, but intended simply to indicate the virtues of cooperation and accord in a perilous situation, and to point out that the courts of Vienna, London, Berlin, and St. Petersburg had great influence. He mentioned also that it was perfectly reasonable for governments guaranteeing a state's neutrality to exert influence in its behalf. The Belgian foreign minister then turned the conversation to specific factors regarding Belgian relations with France. He noted that relations of all sorts were still going on. Commerce was continuing. There had, after all, been a change only in the form of the French government – there was not a new country. Perhaps of more importance was the urgency of the moment and d'Hoffschmidt recalled to his listener the proximity of Brussels to Paris contrasted with the distance of Brussels from Vienna and Berlin. Woyna left the meeting with the feeling that d'Hoffschmidt had spoken with candor and frankness. Belgium would have relations with France, he reported, that were informal but not official and a dispatch to this effect had been sent to the Prince de Ligne. The Austrian minister took some comfort in believing that the Belgian decision corresponded with the status of Britain's Lord Normanby at Paris.[1]

The British ambassador in Brussels also reported at some length on the matter of Belgian recognition of the Provisional Government. Like Woyna, he tried to convince d'Hoffschmidt that Belgium was moving with undue disregard for the opinion of other states. The foreign minister gave him virtually the same response. Belgium was in an

---

[1] Woyna to Metternich, Mar. 8, 1848, AEV. As it turned out, Woyna was correct in this implied coordination of Belgian and British conduct in Paris. See Ligne. *Souvenirs*, p. 33; and Van de Weyer to d'Hoffschmidt, Mar. 4, 1848, and d'Hoffschmidt to Ligne, Mar. 4, 1848, CNB, I, 79–80, 97–98. There was also the argument that, after all, recognition of the Provisional Government did not mean recognition of the French Republic. Like Great Britain Belgium would wait for the definitive establishment of the government.

exposed position. Further, it was in the interest of other states that Belgium act independently of their policies. Howard de Walden deprecated the precipitation and especially the lack of mutual counselling with Belgium's allies. Such an important measure surely merited careful and confidential discussions. The Provisional Government was just that, hardly *"de facto"* at all. Such speed would only convince the French that they were feared in Belgium and this would harm rather than aid Belgian security. Hedging, d'Hoffschmidt asked what the Belgians were supposed to do if the French sent them an ambassador. The Briton replied that this would be improbable unless they had received encouragement. The meeting ended with the foreign minister promising that the matter would receive full study but that the British should remember Belgium's special conditions. He promised that both the British and Prussian ambassadors would be informed of any positive decision.[1] D'Hoffschmidt then wrote Ligne that his talks with Howard de Walden and with Seckendorff convinced him both Britain and Prussia were opposed to official Belgian relations with the Provisional Government. Ligne was thus to take no definite arrangements without specific instructions.[2]

In three days the British minister reported that by hearsay from his colleagues he had learned that the Belgian government had decided to acknowledge the Provisional Government at once. He assured Palmerston that the Liberal ministers were all aware of British views which were disregarded mainly because of fear. Furthermore the cabinet was under pressure from a number of deputies to do anything necessary to remove hostility on the part of France. Despite this, the radical clubs in Paris could be counted on to send trouble-making emissaries to Brussels, no matter what the formal relations of the two governments were. This report had hardly been written when d'Hoffschmidt, true to his word, sent the British minister the gist of recent messages exchanged between the Prince de Ligne and Lamartine. The French foreign minister had given assurances that passports would not be willfully given to known members of radical clubs. The Belgians attempted to have their agent's actions in Paris resemble that of the British minister there. This realization gave satisfaction to the

---

[1] Walden to Palmerston, Mar. 4, 1848, F.O. 10/137. Indeed, on the 7th, Normanby did not know whether Britain would receive a French diplomat or not, or in what capacity. He had asked Palmerston and was awaiting a reply. See Ligne to d'Hoffschmidt, Mar. 7, 1848, CNB, I, 144–146.
[2] D'Hoffschmidt to Ligne, Mar. 4, 1848, *ibid.*, 96.

ministers to Belgium from Prussia, Austria (confirming Woyna, note on p. 45), and Holland.[1]

Of Austria, Great Britain, and Prussia, the latter seemed the least disturbed at the prospect of hasty Belgian recognition. By the first of March, the Prussian government's general view was that France needed the chance to work out its internal problems peaceably; but, for this, she must abstain from any aggression, especially against Belgium, and the Prussian spokesman in Paris had been informed to this effect. This was, of course, good news for the Belgian government and Nothomb relayed the information promptly.[2] He also reported that d'Arnim had been recalled from Paris, Normanby was rumored leaving and he expected that Austria's minister would likewise depart from the French capitol. Nothomb regarded these recalls as a mistake and discussed them freely with associates in Berlin, contending that mere continuation in Paris really did not imply recognition. Canitz denied that d'Arnim had been recalled; he claimed he had only been ordered to Berlin for consultation and was being replaced *ad interim* by the Count de Hatzfeld.[3] Nothomb wrote on the 8th that Arnim would probably stay in Paris, though the counter-order changing the vacation recall had not yet been sent. In Berlin he reported that many of the ministers of secondary states had been ordered to find out what Prussia was going to do, not in three months but at once, about provisional recognition of the French government.[4]

On March 4, 1848, O'Sullivan wrote to d'Hoffschmidt that the *Gazette de Prusse* reported the Belgian recognition of the French Republic. This was slightly premature, perhaps, but accurate. O'Sullivan had been telling people that Belgium would probably recognize the French

---

[1] Walden to Palmerston, 2 letters on Mar. 7, 1848, F.O. 10/137.

[2] Nothomb to d'Hoffschmidt, Mar. 2, 1848, AEB, Pr., IX, This word was also well-received in London. See Van de Weyer to d'Hoffschmidt, Mar. 4, 1848, CNB, I, 77–78.

[3] Nothomb to d'Hoffschmidt, Mar. 3, 4, 1848, AEB, Pr., IX. Other letters created doubt about Arnim leaving; see Nothomb to d'Hoffschmidt, Mar. 3, 1848, CNB, I, 59–63. The Prince de Ligne asked, on February 29, permission to resign his post but stayed on so that it would not look as though he were abandoning it during a period of danger. See Ligne, *Souvenirs*, pp. 32–33. Also on recalls, see d'Hoffschmidt to Ligne, Mar. 6, 1848, CNB, I, 131–132. There was the further point of not wanting to appear hostile to the new French government. See also Van de Weyer to d'Hoffschmidt, Mar. 9, 1848, *ibid.*, 167. Palmerston advised keeping Ligne in Paris, said Normanby was going to be left there and also thought Arnim's leaving an error. Austria had no desire to intervene in France and decided to follow Britain's example and leave Apponyi in Paris as a chargé. See O'Sullivan to d'Hoffschmidt, Mar. 10, 1848, *ibid.*, 176–177.

[4] Nothomb to d'Hoffschmidt, Mar. 8, 1848, *ibid.*, 152. Ligne's health began to give way under the pressure of events and he stayed on despite the strain. D'Hoffschmidt regarded his staying as essential. See d'Hoffschmidt to Ligne, 2 letters on Mar. 25, 1848, and Ligne to d'Hoffschmidt, Mar. 26, 1848, *ibid.*, 255–258.

government if it were like its predecessor on the matter of treaty recognition. It was his opinion that Europe generally would adopt the same view. Metternich had instructed Apponyi to concert with his colleagues and he reminded d'Hoffschmidt of the obvious, that Britain's action would influence a number of others.[1]

On March 4, d'Hoffschmidt informed Nothomb and other Belgian ambassadors of the resolution to recognize the French Republic at an appropriate time. Stressing Belgium's dangerous position, Lamartine's guarantee, and the treaties of 1839, he instructed Nothomb to inform the Prussian Government. The next day d'Hoffschmidt wrote to the main Belgian legations that he had explained Belgium's decision to the ambassadors of Austria,[2] Britain, Holland, and Prussia. He recapitulated how they had brought up the wisdom and propriety of reestablishing diplomatic relations with France before concerting with Belgium's allies and before knowing the decision of the Northern Courts. D'Hoffschmidt claimed that the answer to such a statement was simple: when the French had recognized the treaty of 1839, she became as much an ally as the others and while she continued to abide by the treaty, her particular government was really not a matter for formal Belgian concern. This was certainly an independent statement and perhaps encouraged by the remark of William II of Holland to General Willmar, Belgium's ambassador to Holland, that he intended to "marcher d'accord" with Belgium.[3]

Another encouraging factor was the first formal interview between the Prince de Ligne and Lamartine. This was on March 5 and Lamartine was explicit on the subject of Belgian independence and neutrality.[4] Copies of Ligne's report of this interview were sent by d'Hoffschmidt to Van de Weyer, O'Sullivan, Nothomb, and Willmar. Since Belgium's situation required prompt decision, the government had decided on informal relations since Lamartine said officially that he would respect Belgian neutrality and nationality.[5] From Berlin on March 4,

[1] O'Sullivan to d'Hoffschmidt, Mar. 4, 1848, *ibid.*, 81–82.

[2] Woyna was allowed to have copies of Ligne to d'Hoffschmidt, Feb. 29, 1848, and the response of Mar. 4, 1848, with confidential instructions regarding the renewal of Belgian relations with France. He got these on the promise he would allow only Metternich to see them. This obligation kept him from an entirely frank discussion of the problem with his colleagues from Holland and Prussia with whom he was otherwise on terms of great confidence. See Woyna to Metternich, Mar. 5, 1848, in AEV. Circular letter by d'Hoffschmidt on Mar. 4, 1848, CNB, I, 89–92.

[3] D'Hoffschmidt to Nothomb, Mar. 4 and 2 letters on Mar. 5, 1848, AEB, Pr., IX. Letter of the 5th to the various legations also in CNB, I, 119–120.

[4] D'Hoffschmidt to Nothomb, Mar. 6, 1848, AEB, Pr., IX. Ligne, *Souvenirs*, pp. 73–74; and Ligne to d'Hoffschmidt, Mar. 5, 1848, CNB, I, 108–118.

[5] D'Hoffschmidt to Van de Weyer, O'Sullivan, Nothomb, and Willmar, Mar. 7, 1848, *ibid.*, 149–151.

Nothomb reported a recommendation that Belgium arm moderately, although the danger was more from propaganda than outright war. Prussian spokesmen recommended friendly terms with France and a reliance on Britain.[1] On the 6th Nothomb reported that his colleagues understood Belgium's true motives in the decision. On the 10th d'Hoffschmidt wrote to Nothomb that both Metternich and Palmerston approved Belgium's course regarding France and the declaration by Lamartine tended to prove the wisdom of the action.[2] This was, to say the least, an overstatement of the case since from talks with Seckendorff, Howard de Walden reported to Palmerston that Prussia really deprecated Belgium's early action regarding France. He concluded that the ministers in Brussels of Austria, Prussia, and Holland all wished Belgium would act in concert with British policy rather than separate from it.[3] However, though these ministers spoke with unanimity, Woyna may not have been accurately expressing the views of his government. Metternich had immediately recognized the international dangers of events in Paris, and gave the impression on March 3 that the Austrian policy would be to maintain diplomatic relations with the new government and to consider it bound by existing treaties. In effect, then, this amounted to *de facto* recognition of the Provisional Government; and Count Ficquelmont, Austria's foreign minister, indicated that formal official communication would be resumed as soon as the French had formed a regular government.[4] From Holland Willmar wrote encouragingly that all in the diplomatic corps there approved Belgian informal relations with France.[5]

In Russia word of Louis Philippe's fall occasioned as much dismay and concern as elsewhere. The French chargé d'affaires at St. Petersburg, Count de Rayneval, learned of the revolution while he was entertaining. He was completely taken aback when his secretary abruptly

---

[1] Nothomb to d'Hoffschmidt, Mar. 4, 1848, *ibid.*, 82–87.

[2] Nothomb to d'Hoffschmidt, Mar. 6, 1848, and d'Hoffschmidt to Nothomb, Mar. 10, 1848, AEB, Pr. IX. Van de Weyer reported approval by Palmerston and Prussia's ambassador in London of the instructions sent to Ligne and also that Palmerston and Brunnow agreed that neutrality was the only possible base for Belgian policy. See Van de Weyer to d'Hoffschmidt, Mar. 5, 8, 1848, CNB, I, 99–100, 159–160.

[3] Walden to Palmerston, Mar. 12, 1848, F.O. 10/137. Prussia herself wanted to concert with Britain in her attutide towards the Provisional Government and the British welcomed this, though they would not go so far as to contract a new alliance, in the judgment of Van de Weyer. See Van de Weyer to d'Hoffschmidt, Mar. 8, 1848, CNB, I, 162.

[4] Ponsonby to Palmerston, Mar. 1, 3, 7, 20, 1848, F.O. 10/137. The King of Prussia sent General Radowitz to Vienna to confer on general European problems and there were communications with Nicholas I. Ponsonby expected quick agreement among the three powers and that in the talks, Austria would be firmly for non-intervention in French internal affairs.

[5] Willmar to d'Hoffschmidt, Mar. 10, 1848, CNB, I, 175.

walked in and declared, "Citizen of France, the Republic is declared." [1] The Tsar heard the news with "le plus grand calme." He said that France was free to regulate its own internal affairs but that he would join his allies to repel any infraction of treaties and the French chargé was so informed. A million rubles was put immediately at the disposal of the war minister, a large sum considering the Empire's known financial condition.[2]

In London the Russian ambassador, Baron de Brunnow, was suggesting that possibly the time had come to consider occupying Belgium's fortresses facing the French frontier. Van de Weyer reported this to d'Hoffschmidt who at once forwarded the message to Nothomb in Berlin. Since Russia still had no direct diplomatic contact with the Belgian government, communication was indirect and obscure. Nothomb was emphatic in calling Brunnow's ideas clearly inopportune. In Berlin he reported the current feeling that a great mistake had been made in 1815 by deciding to build a line of fortresses parallel to the French frontier. Instead, it was now agreed that the line of the Escaut and Meuse was the proper defensive location, with the highest priority being placed on the defense of Antwerp.[3] Other than this word regarding defenses, the Belgians received no word from the Russians. There was the implication that the Russians would regard French aggression with alarm even though they still did not recognize Belgium. There was no hint whatever from the Russians regarding the pros and cons of early Belgian recognition of the Provisional Government.

The French ambassador in Brussels had been the Marquis de Rumigny. His post was taken over on March 12, 1848, by Sérurier, who

[1] Georgiana Bloomfield, *Re miniscences of Court and Diplomatic Life* (London, 1883), p. 170

[2] Nothomb to d'Hoffschmidt, Mar. 14, 1848, AEB, Pr., IX. Nicholas shortly wrote to Victoria suggesting (while congratulating her on the birth of a daughter, Louise, Mar. 18) that the union of Britain and Russia discussed in 1844 was now vitally needed for European stability; Nicholas to Victoria, 22 Mar. – 3 April, 1848, LV, II, 196.

[3] Van de Weyer to d'Hoffschmidt, Mar. 6, 1848 (copy to Nothomb, AEB, Pr.,I X, also in CNB, I, 124–126) and Nothomb to d'Hoffschmidt, Mar. 11, 1848, also CNB, I, 184–185. See also Van de Weyer to d'Hoffschmidt, Mar. 8, 1848, *ibid.*, 157–159. Van de Weyer discussed these ideas of Brunnow with Palmerston who also regarded them as inopportune. Bunsen and Dietrichstein told Brunnow they would do nothing without consulting Van de Weyer who in turn told them Belgium could and would defend itself. Brunnow then said the Belgian dispositions were wise but that Belgium really should not move without concert with other powers. Austria, Britain, Prussia, and Russia should discuss any changes, especially questions regarding saving or demolishing particular fortresses. Van de Weyer saw in all this the beginning of a vast coalition against France. D'Hoffschmidt approved Van de Weyer's handling of Brunnow's embarrassing suggestion. See d'Hoffschmidt to Van de Weyer, Mar. 10, 1848, *ibid.*, 170–171. See the earlier Secret Memo of the ambassadors of the Northern Powers (p. 1 of this chapter, note 4 and material it supports). From London Van de Weyer reported that Prussia was not supporting Brunnow on the question of the Belgian fortresses; Van de Weyer to d'Hoffschmidt, Mar. 21, 1848, *ibid.*, 231–232.

was accredited as provisionally charged with the administration of the affairs of the Republic in Belgium. In his first meeting with d'Hoffschmidt he claimed that France wanted to be a good neighbor and wished a relationship that was loyal and simple. The foreign minister replied in like language and expressed Belgium's hope that the Provisional Government could consolidate the work it had so courageously begun; this was essential for the repose of both France and Europe. Lamartine's name, he explained, was regarded by Belgians and others as a guarantee of order and dignity. He explained Belgian efforts at increasing armaments after clamors for economy had earlier reduced them. Belgium needed more force to insure respect for her neutrality. Forts were being repaired and armed on all frontiers and there was absolutely no hostile intent regarding France. Sérurier was convinced of d'Hoffschmidt's frankness. He indicated that the policies of the Belgian government were wise and gave assurances that the French completely approved.[1] D'Hoffschmidt, gratified by Sérurier's language, confided to Britain's ambassador that Sérurier's being sent to Brussels, rather than an obviously avid republican, meant a future with a minimum of inconveniences and annoyance.[2] Thus appropriate Franco-Belgian relations were established, "officieuses" but not "officielles."

[1] Sérurier to Lamartine, Mar. 13, 1848, AEF, Belg., XXX; also in DD, I, 182–183.
[2] Walden to Palmerston, Mar. 11, 13, 14, 1848, F.O. 10/139.

CHAPTER VI

BELGIAN INTERNAL REACTION TO THE FEBRUARY REVOLUTION

In the face of circumstances reminiscent of the thirties, the crown and cabinet were drawn closer together. On February 25, Leopold wrote to Charles Rogier, advising prudence and careful surveillance, since revolutionary clubs in Paris might cause trouble. By all means the frontier must be watched, especially near Lille.[1] Rogier sent a circular to all provincial governors on February 26, warning of the serious situation and advising that strangers should have passports checked with care. On March 2, another circular authorized the start of as many public works as possible, since steady employment might ease the period of crisis.[2] Meanwhile, Chazal had given assurances that the frontiers were ready for defence.[3] All these precautions, however, supplemented a general policy of hospitality and welcome to strangers whose papers were in order and whose stated objectives were not to create disorder.[4] Obviously, the border watch was only to be effective against an open attack; otherwise entry into Belgium was fairly easy.

Almost any word of serious difficulty would not have surprised the Liberal ministry late in February; but, for the moment, Brussels was quiet and there were grounds for hope in Lamartine's first message to the Prince de Ligne. Public sentiment was reassuring as some democratic agitation merely attracted ridicule.[5] Rather than hopes of imitating the French example, there was a sense of disgust.[6] Meanwhile from the French capitol, via Normanby, Palmerston, and Van de Weyer, came the confidential but comforting word that the Provisional

---

[1] Leopold to Rogier, Feb. 25, 1848, RP, 107.
[2] Bertrand, *Démocratie*, I, 287–289; and Discailles, *Rogier*, III, 236–237.
[3] Chazal to d'Hoffschmidt, [Feb.] 1848, DM, V.
[4] HP, II, 662–663.
[5] Van Praet to Van de Weyer, Feb. 29, 1848, VWP, 274; and Woyna to Metternich, Feb. 29, 1848, AEV. Anti-French and anti-republican sentiment led to the dissolution of two democratic clubs, one in Brussels and one in Antwerp. See Walden to Palmerston, Apr. 4, 1848, F.O. 10/138.
[6] Waller to Palmerston, Feb. 29, 1848, F.O. 10/137.

Government was resolved to maintain peace with its neighbors and specifically had no wish to annex Belgium.[1] On the other hand, three different authors, all writing letters from Paris on the 26th, reported that "the great news of the day" was the abdication of King Leopold and the proclamation of a republic at Brussels.[2]

It was only a matter of days before the apprehensions of Belgian leaders proved justified. For Belgium the past was entirely too close at hand; too many aspects of the *status quo* of 1847 were too recently arrived at; and nationalism was particularly a potentially disruptive force in this borderland area.

Brabant was relatively undisturbed by events in Paris. In Louvain the garrison encouraged stability and the burgomaster reported a rare cry of "Vive la République!" and that all would go well as long as Brussels was calm. Brussels itself was particularly quiet considering that it was the nation's capitol, although occasionally some voice might be heard calling for a republic – and journals exaggerated these. At word of revolution in Paris many members of the two liberal societies of Brussels (representing a split in liberal ranks into the Alliance and the more moderate Liberal and Constitutional Association) cooperated. Some Frenchmen bent on subversion through the Alliance were rudely received and met with no success. The two conspirators, Blervacq and Fosse, who worked to overthrow the regime after finding support in Paris, distrusted each other, Fosse regarding Blervacq as ultra radical while Blervacq accused Fosse of really wanting to see an Orangist restoration. The Democratic Association, founded in November, 1847, contained a host of alien radicals later expelled by the government. All the provinces had democratic and republican associations modeled on Brussels; and by the end of 1848, all main cities and towns had at least one such organization and Brussels had four. Despite active government supervision, their press proliferated markedly in 1848. Before February 24, the membership in these groups was mostly bourgeoisie with a few workers. Fourierism was strong and Brussels was a center of international socialism as well, Karl Marx himself working in Brussels. After February 24, a distinct effort was made to attract more workers into the radical movements. After debating its proper role in the crisis, the Democratic Association sent agents to Paris, appealing to Belgians there to organize and bring republicanism

[1] Palmerston to Van de Weyer, Feb. 29, 1848, VWP, 116.
[2] Cara[s] (at Ypres) to Rogier, Feb. 28, 1848, RP, 74; and Bronne, *Jules Van Praet*, p. 36. The Prince de Ligne reported this rumor (CNB, I, 24–26) to d'Hoffschmidt on Feb. 29, 1848; he did not happen to hear it until the morning of the 29th.

to Belgium. Meanwhile the Association caused many domestic disturbances. There is no doubt that their object was the establishment of
a republic in Belgium. Some of the more republican members of the
Alliance who supported this, immediately lost popular support. One
segment was cooperating with a group in Amsterdam, trying unsuccessfully to organize a common popular uprising in both capitols.
Jottrand was their candidate to head a provisional government in
Brussels. While the Rogier ministry took appropriate extra security
measures, especially in areas frequented by the king, the financial structure caused the greatest source of alarm. Leopold was counseling that
nothing be done to cause a panic; everyone must be allowed to share
in the general well-being and the greatest efforts made to maintain
the level of employment.[1]

In Luxemburg province, March and April were months of marked
uneasiness. Just across the southern border in France, enthusiastic
demonstrations celebrated events in Paris; and rumors drifted north-
ward that Belgian workers were being expelled from France.[2] This
word, confirmed by March 8, led to local demands that non-Belgians
be discharged. Work stoppages in Bertrix and Herbeumont left over
three hundred workers unemployed. Governor Smits felt that, for the
moment, public works would meet the temporary needs of this group
and thus avoid a public disturbance.[3] By mid-March, a hundred and
fifty workers from France had arrived near Battincourt. Smits reported
that while the demonstrations now favored country, king, and bishop,
it was urgent that work be found. In the Grand Duchy on the eastern
boundary of the province, the repercussions of events in Paris were
more serious. Smits worried about what would happen if a republic
were declared there and appealed for more armed strength for his province. On March 20, Chazal informed Rogier that artillery from Liège

---

[1] Liedts to Rogier, Mar. 3, 4, 1848, RP, 74. Liedts included reports from subordinate
officials; Rogier forwarded the lot to Chazal. Included was the comment that a few volunteer
groups had been organized but that no arms were available to them. The almost daily
reports in Feb. and Mar., 1848, from Liège reported general quiet, these also in RP, 74.
See also Leopold to Rogier, Mar. 18, 1848, RP, 107; Willmar to d'Hoffschmidt, Mar. 26,
1848, CNB, I, 257–258; Van Praet to Van de Weyer, Mar. 1, 2, 4, 5, 7, 9, May 6, 17, 1848,
VWP, 274; *The Economist*, July 22, 1848; Pierre de la Gorce, *Histoire de la Seconde République Française* (2 vols., Paris, 1925), I, 182; Bertrand, *Démocratie*, I, 204–207, 257–268,
309–315, 318, 329–357, 413–446; Woyna to Metternich, Mar. 16, 1848, AEV; Walden to
Palmerston, Mar. 18, 1848, and Waller to Palmerston, Feb. 27, 1848, F.O. 10/137. The
Observateur, Feb. 27, 1848, carried a statement of the sentiments of advanced liberals then
in Brussels.
[2] Smits to Rogier, Mar. 3, 4, 5, 1848, RP, 74. For a more expanded account, based largely
on the Rogier Papers, see Jules Garsou, "La Révolution de 1848 dans le Luxembourg belge,"
in *Carnet de la Fourragère* (1933), 270–291, 351–364.
[3] Smits to Rogier, Mar. 7, 8, 1848, RP, 74.

and infantry from Namur were being moved to reinforce points in Luxemburg. On the 19th, a red flag was flying in the frontier village of Virton.[1] Two days later Smits wrote of a "vast conspiracy" which he believed would soon attempt to join the populations of the two Luxemburgs (Grand Duchy and Belgian province) – thus destroying the settlement of 1839. He described, on the 25th, how one possibility for a new order envisaged a union of the Belgian and Germanic Luxemburgs into a separate nation. Clearly, he believed, Belgian armed force would be needed in such a contingency. The governor suspected treason and that his reports to Rogier were being intercepted. On the 26th, he wrote of pillaging and unrest in many areas and renewed his plea for more military force.[2]

Within the Grand Duchy many who wished a union with Belgium and a complete break with the Dutch monarch were naming deputies to the Belgian Chamber. Smits believed that William II could save his duchy only by immediate approval and establishment of a customs union between the Grand Duchy and Belgium. This, however, must be done at once and Smits feared that events were marching too swiftly perhaps even for this. In Arlon *l'Echo du Luxembourg* urged that the Luxemburgers, separated since 1839, should now be reunited entirely within Belgium.[3] At the end of March Smits reported general quiet but widespread agitation in the Grand Duchy. He had argued with those favoring a large Luxemburg within Belgium, especially on grounds that Belgian independence depended on its being neutral and *non-conquering*. The French reaction to such a realignment was particularly to be feared. Smits worried about hostile bands near Sedan and Carignan; and with fresh rumors of an armed band coming from Paris, a few more French flag plantings, and with business slowing up in Arlon, he requested an additional credit from the government. At virtually the same time, Rogier , in response to Smits' letter of the 25th, emphasized the same view that Smits had argued, that treaties made a neutral

---

[1] Smits to Rogier, Mar. 16, 17, 19, 20, 1848, and Chazal to Rogier, Mar. 20, 1848, *ibid.* Smits had only 14 gendarmes (10 mounted), 600 infantry, and a bourgeois guard which he regarded as feebly organized.

[2] Smits to Rogier, Mar. 21, 26, 1848, *ibid.*; and Smits to Rogier, Mar. 25, 1848, DM, V, with a Mar. 25 copy of *L'Echo du Luxembourg* (Arlon).

[3] Smits to Rogier, Mar. 28, 29, 1848, RP, 74. On March 27, Nothomb wrote that if a joining of the two Luxemburgs were attempted, German troops would be sent to the Grand Duchy and that Belgian relations would be compromised with both Germany and the King Grand Duke. From Holland, on April 4, Willmar reported general ignorance of the situation in the Grand Duchy, though at least one person in the grand ducal government regarded the ducal crown as in danger. From his inquiries, Willmar gathered that a myriad of possibilities existed; Luxemburg with France, Luxemburg with Belgium, Belgian Luxemburg with Luxemburg, etc. See CNB, I, 260–261, 329–332.

country of Belgium and that, however much Belgians might sympa-
thize with their former brothers, they must resist offers of union, since
any questions which tended toward a redrawing of boundaries could
only serve to weaken the country's position.[1] During the first week of
April, 1848, the situation was alleviated somewhat when politicians
in the Grand Duchy looked eastward, discussion centering on the idea
of a customs union with German states. Now there was general quiet
within the province, though rumors persisted of roving bands across
the French frontier.[2] During this period Rogier had sent as much
help to Smits as he could and the governor was duly appreciative.
There were, however, other voices. Arlon's *l'Echo du Luxembourg* and
l'Observateur du Luxembourg at Neufchâteau charged that the government had done nothing for the province, had resisted measures favorable to the area, and was in fact hostile to Luxemburg. In the Grand
Duchy the *Courier du Grand-Duché de Luxembourg* carried an editorial
on April 1, that noted Rogier's "cruel adieu" implied by Belgium's
wish to stand simply for order and industry.[3] Across the French border
near Sedan there was disorder from undisciplined bands and another
red flag was found at Virton. From Paris came a Mr. Hourry, a Luxem-
burger by birth, whose idea was that the province and Grand Duchy
unite into an independent republic as a protectorate under France.
Unable to gain a following, he returned to Paris.[4]

Meanwhile, the Prince de Ligne was worried about the situation in
Luxemburg and at his urging, d'Hoffschmidt wrote to Rogier about
forming a volunteer civic guard near Luxemburg to prevent bands of
people from taking justice into their own hands.[5] Smits turned down
a leave offered him on April 20 because of the gravity of the situation
in the Grand Duchy. While he saw a peaceful solution there, he saw
other horrifying prospects as more likely. The least incident there could
cause an explosion, as he saw it, and he was particularly apprehensive regarding both the proclamation of an independent republic and the infla-
matory writings of Baron de Blockhauzen. In terms of troops, Smits felt
he was in a very difficult position, with barely enough in Arlon to main-

---

[1] Smits to Rogier, Mar. 30, 1848, RP, 74. Smits to Rogier, Mar. 29, 31, 1848, and Rogier
to [Smits], Mar. 29 (or 30), 1848, DM, V.

[2] Smits to Rogier, Apr. 1, 2, 3, 5, 6, 7, 1848, RP, 74.

[3] Smits to Rogier, Apr. 8, 9, 1848, *ibid.*

[4] Smits to Rogier, Apr. 9, 11, 1848, *ibid.*; and Smits to Rogier, Mar. 25, 1848, DM, V.

[5] D'Hoffschmidt to Rogier, Apr. 18, 1848, RP, 126. Smits was keeping d'Hoffschmidt
informed of reports he sent regarding neighboring countries. He also had pressed on Charles
Rogier the need for more strength, especially a mobile column of infantry and cavalry.
See Smits to d'Hoffschmidt, Apr. 21, 1848, and Smits to Rogier, Apr. 21, 1848, DM, V.

tain control over his own population.[1] For the time being his apprehensions were put to rest as the last half of April witnessed a tentative
solution to the immediate problem in the Grand Duchy. Though there
still remained those favoring union with Belgium, an agreement was
reached which took the Belgian constitution as a basis for a new Grand
Ducal constitution. The Duchy became generally quiet; while just to
the east, Trier was in full insurrection. In the province, Virton again
attracted the governor's attention, as an anonymous placard threatened both the burgomaster and the commissaire d'arrondissement.[2] With
stability in the Grand Duchy, the danger of insurrection was over; and
Smits was sure he would maintain order if nothing too radical happened
in France.[3]

As it turned out, there had been little real danger of trouble
from within Luxemburg province.[4] A republican flag here or
a radical there could be dealt with and political appeal from the outside
met with no widespread response within the province. There is virtually
no evidence to suggest anything but indifference, except in cases where
people were unemployed. The frustations from 1839 appear to have
been much more acute in the Luxemburg left outside Belgium than
in the Belgian province.

The province of Namur was generally quiet after the revolution in
Paris. There were apprehensions of trouble, however, especially along
the southern frontier facing France. The French frontier villages of
Givet, Rocroi, and Charleville were calm in early March and Rogier
received from Vrière, the new governor in Namur, reassurances that
all was well in the province and that what was only "yesterday a political duty" forced by circumstances was now a genuine devotion to the
king.[5] Namur was, of course, a center of royalist strength. On March 10,
Vrière reported a petition being circulated by a Mr. Burck (whom
Vrière felt should be expelled) demanding the reunion of Belgium and
France.[6] There were also further disquieting reports. From Brûly,

[1] Smits to Rogier, Apr. 21, 1848, DM, V.
[2] Smits to Rogier, Apr. 17, 24, 26, 27, 28, 30, May 4, 1848, RP, 74. See also DM, V, entries
250–254, for journals and proclamations relating to the situation in the Grand Duchy late
in April.
[3] Smits to Rogier, May 7, 1848, RP, 74. Ten days later he reported a republican flag raised
at Remick but no trouble.
[4] D'Hoffschmidt to Chazal and also to Smits, Feb. 23, 1849, DM., V. The republican
movement in Belgian Luxemburg was still being closely watched.
[5] Vrière to Rogier, Feb. 28, Mar. 2, 4. 5, 1848, RP, 74.
[6] Vrière to Rogier, Mar. 10, 1848, ibid. Also on Mar. 10, Haussy notified d'Hoffschmidt
(DM, V) that Burck had left for Paris carrying the same (presumably) petition which demanded reunion of the arrondissement of Philippeville with France.

north across the border from Rocroi, came word of loyalty but also of mixed feelings, curiosity and of paying "the French for their descent on Antwerp." [1] In the cities of Namur and Charleroi rumor advised congregating at Brussels.[2] Vrière informed Rogier on March 25, 1848, that a number of radicals who formerly had been cooperating with the moderate liberals, now had decided that the moment of agitation had come. The Liberal Association of Namur was split. Vrière decried the potential loss of liberal influence on the full blown-radicals and, with the moderate faction losing its organ in the local press (since *l'Eclaireur* was now publishing extremely liberal views in the name of "liberal progress"), the danger in the next elections was a defeat for the regular Liberal Party. Also, a pamplet written by a lawyer, Gislain, criticized the dynasty.[3] While there was thus some rumbling in the city of Namur, there was also a petition sent to Rogier and d'Hoffschmidt which asked that all necessary measures be taken to insure the independence of Belgium.[4]

The most potentially explosive place in the province was Mariembourg. Here the population was very much pro-French. Many, including the burgomaster, were proud of having fought under the Empire. They had, in fact, never really regarded themselves as subjects of Belgium. As of late March, most of the city's inhabitants were well-armed and the civic guard of two hundred twenty was regarded as powerless to put down any popular uprising which might take place. Burck and other republicans were in high favor in Mariembourg. A druggist, Buzon, went to Rocroi carrying a petition with names from Mariembourg to the new sous-préfet, requesting the French government to unite with Belgium, forming a single state. Buzon was not well-received at Rocroi and Vrière moved to get a court judgment against him.[5]

[1] Magniette (curé at Brûly) to *commissaire d'arrondissement* at Philippeville, Mar. 20, 1848 (forwarded to Rogier by Vrière on Mar. 25), RP, 74.
[2] Vrière to Rogier, Mar. 10, 1848, *ibid*.
[3] Vrière to Rogier, Mar. 25, 1848, *ibid*.
[4] HP, II, 663; see also, on p. 677, the statement of the Marquis de Rodes in the Senate on Mar. 4, 1848.
[5] Vrière to Rogier, Mar. 22, 25, 1848, RP, 74. On Mar. 17, 1848, Rogier had requested a check on the republican party at Mariembourg. Vrière's letter of Mar. 22, contained local reports which were forwarded, including one from the *commissaire d'arrondissement* at Philippeville to Vrière (Mar. 21) and another from the commanding captain of the gendarmerie at Namur to Vrière (Mar. 22). Also in the Rogier dossier (74) at this point was a report by a major made to the commanding general at Namur. It went through channels (Anoul, Chazal) to Rogier. On local republicans in Mariembourg, it noted their demands for reform and that their goal was the union with France of the cantons which had been detached from France by the treaties of 1815.

On April 8, Vrière wrote of the difficulty of obtaining, without unfavorable publicity, an exact confidential list of the names of workers
entering the province from France.[1] Also in April trouble was anticipate
in Gedinne and Willerzie, south of Dinant. There were demonstrations
and violent assassinations across the border in France (at Autrerivière)
and women talked of going to pillage in Belgium. All this created
unrest in Gedinne; and, though the citizens were unarmed, the
gendarmerie cooperated closely with local authorities, keeping close
watch and making careful patrols of the border.[2] On April 17, rioting
broke out in Couvin south of Mariembourg. Here the city had reduced
the numbers employed in public works. There were cries of "Vive la
République! " but the gendarmerie moved swiftly and restored order,
making only a few arrests.[3] Thus, although Mariembourg was a sensitive place, Namur as a province was generally quiet during March and
April following the February Revolution. Surveillance was, of course,
continued for some time and passports were especially scrutinized.
Military units stood ready to march on short notice from Dinant,
Philippeville, and Namur; and Vrière assured Rogier that any more
bands entering Belgium would be either repulsed or destroyed.[4] In
Mariembourg where sentiment for France was strong, this by itself –
even in the face of some avid republicans – was not enough to cause
open revolt. Trouble in Couvin had been economic in origin and contained by swift action. Latent discontents were not enough to cause
much response to the events in France and the most sensitive areas
were the frontier regions, as might be expected.

To the northeast in the province of Limbourg, March was marked
by general quiet with some word of agitation across the Dutch border,
particularly at Maestricht where the population was distrusted by
the Netherlands government. A project to concentrate some Dutch
troops on the Belgian frontier was cancelled, because such a demonstration would create ill-will and disapproval on both sides of the border.[5]
At Diest some Flemish soldiers reportedly sang Flemish lyrics which
showed disrespect for Leopold. The most serious incidents occurred at
Maeseyck where, during a carnival, there were some cries of "Vive

[1] Vrière to Rogier, Apr. 8, 1848, *ibid.*

[2] Reports from burgomaster of Willerzie to brigade commander of the gendarmerie at
Gedinne, Apr. 4, 1848, and from the commander of the gendarmerie for the province to
Vrière, Apr. 7, 1848 (both forwarded by Vrière to Rogier), *ibid.*

[3] Gendarmerie brigade commander at Couvin to his headquarters at Namur, Apr. 17,
1848 (forwarded by Vrière to Rogier, Apr. 21, 1848), *ibid.*

[4] Vrière to Rogier, July 3, 1848, *ibid.*

[5] D'Hoffschmidt to Chazal, Mar. 2, 1848, DM, V.

la République! " which received no response and signalled no disorder.
Also at Maeseyck a placard appeared demanding recall of city officials,
but these actions were characterized as of little importance by Limbourg's governor, Schiervel, in his reports to Rogier.[1] In April and
May there was some excitement but mostly across the border. Trouble
broke out in Maestricht; and at Thorn, just over the frontier from
Maeseyck, shots were exchanged between the gendarmerie and the
citizenry. The frontier was closely watched and songs were heard
asking union with Belgium. In May, flags of the Germanic Confeder-
ation were flying in a number of insurgent communes and people were
saying that Prussia would annex the province. At Eysdem, the Prussian flag flew only briefly, as the gendarmerie from Maestricht came
and took it down. In Maestricht, some people insisted that they had
no desire to remain Hollandais and were going to Cologne to ask annexation to Prussia.[2] For Limbourg, therefore, the situation was
somewhat analogous to that in Luxemburg province as far as the question of nationalism was concerned. What danger there was stemmed
from the action of malcontents resident outside of Belgium proper.

In Antwerp there was no sign of agitation following the upheaval in
Paris and a careful surveillance of strangers and the frontier proved
hardly necessary. There were, of course, rumors leading to stock
fluctuations as well as the problem of work stoppages and of men consequently unemployed. A group of such workers gathered on the morning
of March 22 at the house of Antwerp's burgomaster, Gerard Legrelle,
who told them to disband and that the city government had always
done all it could in the manner of employment. The workers left after
stating that they only wanted work and food; that having no bread,
they were asking the authorities for work. Two days later they appeared
again in large numbers but dispersed quietly with no police action
necessary. To prevent the situation from deteriorating, the city officials
decided, on their own, to start work at once on an infantry caserne, a
hospital, and a harbor quai, though aid was hoped for from the ministry
of public works.[3] Late in April, Rogier, after a query about how the
king would be received if he were to visit, was assured that in Antwerp
both the king and his government were symbols of order, repose, and

---

[1] Schiervel to Rogier, Mar. 3, 4, 5, 6, 7, 8, 10, 23, 1848, RP, 74.

[2] Schiervel to Rogier, Apr. 5, 10, 1848, *ibid.*; gendarmerie captain at Liège to colonel
commanding at Brussels, May 15, 1848; and gendarmerie lieutenant at Tongres to colonel
commanding at Brussels, May 12, 15, 1848, DM, V. See also Schiervel to Rogier, Apr. 4,
1848, *ibid.*, for minor violence and bloodshed in Limbourg communes of Herlen and Vaels.

[3] Delecke to Rogier, Mar. 2, 3, 4, 22, 24, 1848, RP, 74; and Waller to Palmerston, Feb.
27, 1848, F.O. 10/137.

tranquillity, and that Leopold would be enthusiastically welcomed.[1]

The province of Hainaut numbered among those where the danger
was potentially acute. Across the border in Lille, the French army was
maintaining patrols and guards were seen on every hand. The National
Guard was also cooperating and morale was high in both groups. While
violence by the populace was no problem in Lille, careful surveillance
was maintained, largely on the initiative of local commanders (Generals
de Négrier and de Golstein) who were without official news from Paris
and highly sceptical of most accounts which they believed were exaggerated.[2] In Hainaut precautions were taken. A veritable invasion
of propagandists was anticipated and all the burgomasters prepared to
watch and arrest the expected strangers. In Mons the events of Paris
made a profound impression but the population showed no desire
to follow such an example. On February 27, 1848, Governor Dumon
Dumortier confidentially reported quiet and his opinion that in France
the revolution appeared to be vague and indecisive, thus giving a
chance for monarchists and also the provinces to play a part yet in
deciding the destiny of France.[3] By March 4, Hainaut was still calm
but again the economic problem entered the picture as Dumortier
foresaw danger should money for railway construction be discon-
tinued. A line being built from Jurbise to Tournai was being financed
by money from Britain. The next day his apprehension moved nearer
to reality as the funds stopped coming and work was immediately
suspended. Appeals to the banks at Mons, Tournai, and Charleroi were
refused.[4] Other sectors of the province also faced similar dangers. At
Soignies on March 11, a crisis was regarded as imminent if remedial
measures were not instituted to alleviate the slowdown of work in the
major industries. At St. Denis the labor of three hundred men had
already been restricted and from Charleroi came the same sort of
complaint, also with pleas for aid to local industry. "Continued employment is the safeguard of public order" was Dumortier's sober
conclusion. Work on the Tournai-Jurbise line was started up but this
was inadequate to meet the province-wide decline. The workers generally
were understanding and, for the short run, prepared to accept their
misfortune as simply part of a larger financial crisis which they apparently did not expect local authorities to be able to cope

[1] Delecke to Rogier, Apr. 27, 1848, RP, 126.
[2] Van der W[eyde] to Rogier, Feb. 26, 27, 1848, RP, 74.
[3] Dumon Dumortier to Rogier, Feb. 27, 1848, *ibid.*
[4] Dumortier to Rogier, Mar. 4, 5, 7, *ibid.*

with.[1] In the midst of this unemployment problem in Hainaut, danger materialized directly from France. A gendarmerie report (March 11) stated that between four and five hundred Belgian workers were leaving Paris by rail and planning to go to Brussels "to cause trouble there." The report for March 12 was more precise and even more disturbing. There was a legion of Belgian workers, three thousand strong, who were expecting to find arms at Lille before entering Belgium near Mouseron. These reports came simultaneously with reassurances from Tournai where despite a few known republicans, all was quiet.[2]

The movement of troops to Courtrai from the garrison at Tournai gave pause to the colonel commanding at Tournai.[3] Most of March passed with only minor incidents – local commanders took what precautions they could and, like the commissaire d'arrondissement at Ath, waited in anticipation of trouble from workers being expelled from France.[4] On the 28th and 29th, disturbances occurred at Vaulx, Antoing, Chercq, Wasmes, and Pâturages and at other points in the province. The rioters were generally outsiders aided by republicans and met with little response from the workers whose morale was surprisingly good. Dumortier recommended sending arms to a number of communes where the "friends of order" were unarmed. The menace came from bands of fifteen to twenty crossing the frontier from France. At the same time, *La Gazette de Mons*, despite its liberal background and indirect advice from Dumortier, was publishing articles promoting republicanism; indeed it carried completely opposing ideas in the same issue.[5]

The first week in April was one of unrest and potential danger. Money for continued employment became scarcer and small bands of unemployed Belgians forcefully expelled from France, spreading stories of utopian republicanism, made local officials uneasy. Their task was made more difficult by violence to the west in West Flanders.

---

[1] Dumon Dumortier to Rogier, Mar. 13, 14, 1848, *ibid.* Letter of Mar. 13, enclosed reports made to him by his *commissaire d'arrondissement*. Letter of Mar. 14, enclosed report to him by burgomaster of Charleroi, Mar. 12, 1848. Quote is from this latter.

[2] Gendarmerie reports (Mar. 11, 12) of Captain Pire of the brigade at Quiévrain, forwarded to Rogier, Mar. 12, 1848, *ibid.* These reported identity of leaders of the legion. See also R. Dumortiez (colonel commanding civic guard at Tournai) to Rogier, Mar. 12, 1848, *ibid.* Walden reported (to Palmerston Mar. 27, 1848, F. O. 10/137) cooperation by Delescluze, who warned Belgian authorities of the approach of the legion and promised his cooperation. Woyna, Walden, and Sérurier all kept their respective governments abreast of reports of the legion which were circulating in Brussels. See also *The Economist*, Apr. 1, 8, 1848; and Ligne's report to d'Hoffschmidt, Mar. 10, 1848, CNB, I, 179–180, which was particularly accurate.

[3] R. Dumortiez to Rogier, Mar. 17, 1848, RP, 74.

[4] *Commissaire d'arrondissement* at Ath to Rogier, Mar. 27, 1848, *ibid.*

[5] Dumon Dumortier to Rogier, Mar. 30, 31, 1848, *ibid.*

Public works on the local scene were promoted as much as possible and rigorous surveillance by the army combined to prevent complete disorder.[1] A number of republican agitators in a demonstration at Quiévrain planted a tree of liberty on the frontier. Alert action by the communal administration prevented this from getting out of hand. May was generally quiet; but in June, with the problem of finance coinciding with local elections, Dumortier foresaw a grand opportunity for trouble makers. While explaining the possibilities to Rogier, he pointed out the personal financial sacrifice he was incurring for having accepted the governorship of Hainaut.[2] Late in June a special alert followed reports of new bands of insurgents coming from Paris. Cavalry was sent to Beaumont and the garrisons near Chimay ordered to be ready to move at an instant's notice. Garrisons were also alerted at nearby Philippeville and Mariembourg in the province of Namur. The problem of defense against armed insurgents was not basically the problem in Hainaut; for, as Dumortier pointed out to Rogier, the big question was what to do about men – fellow Belgians mostly – fleeing France by compulsion and lacking passports. Dumortier felt that "our institutions" opposed turning them away and yet in Hainaut, as in the rest of Belgium, there was no employment at hand for them.[3]

Of all the provinces in Belgium, probably the reports from West Flanders caused the greatest concern for Rogier. The governor, like those of other provinces, reported to Rogier almost daily and instructed his burgomasters to take precautionary measures. The lace industry was severely hit by conditions in France but all was so calm in the province initially that by March 9, day by day reports appeared no longer necessary. Unemployment at Ypres and Bruges created unrest but the frontier was peaceful: the only sign of trouble came from two drunks; one calling for the prompt union of Belgium and France, the other shouting simply, "Vive la République!"[4] From the 12th of March on, the reports grew more ominous. Lace workers at Menin were especially restive. In Bruges, a twenty-nine year old shoemaker, recently arrived from Paris, told stories of Belgians in Paris who were

---

[1] Dumon Dumortiez to Rogier, Apr. 3, 4, 7, 8, 9, 1848, *ibid*. The maintenance of the troops was itself an additional hardship on local inhabitants.

[2] Dumon Dumortier to Rogier, Apr. 13, 14, 15, 19, June 4, 1848, *ibid*. Letter of Apr. 19, forwarded a report from V. Misson to Dumon Dumortier, Apr. 18, 1848.

[3] Dumon Dumortier to Rogier, July 1, 3, 1848; gendarmerie brigade commander at Couvin to colonel commanding at Brussels, June 30, 1848; the sous prefect of Rocroi to burgomaster of Chimay, June 30, 1848; and report no. 289 of the gendarmerie brigade commander at Chimay, June 30, 1848, *ibid*.

[4] Gov. of W. Flanders (Bruges) to Rogier, Feb. 26, 27. Mar. 4 (2), 5. 6, 7, 8, 9, 1848, *ibid*.

being led by a former colonel, a large corpulent person, and a young lawyer of twenty-five or twenty-seven years. He did not know their names. Rumors reached Bruges of disorder in Menin, but no official word. Troops arrived at Courtrai. From Ypres the burgomaster, Alphonse Vandenpeereboom, emphasized the growing unrest. He pictured the misery of the working class increasing by the day and insisted that it was urgent that the government intervene at once. A storehouse, partially filled with potatoes scheduled for export to Britain, required special police protection.[1] On the 16th Vandenpeereboom reported an adverse reaction to a decision by Chazal to use troops in construction work in new fortifications. Should this decision be carried out, he was convinced there would be trouble between the troops and the bourgeoisie. There was already talk of more work if Belgium were part of France; and, what with current news of troubles (perhaps exaggerated) at Bruges and Ghent, the situation required great care and wisdom.[2]

In Bruges crowds gathered in the Grand Place on March 14, 15, and 16. They were generally peaceable and the police had little difficulty dispersing them. From Lille, on the 15th, came word that Ernest Grégoire, "commanding the Belgian company at Lille," was leading a band of eighteen hundred Belgian workers en route to proclaim the republic in Belgium. The frontiers now were alerted. Belgian and French Comines were, in effect, one town with a bridge as the dividing line. Here some people crossed into Belgian Comines, shouted, "Vive la République!" and then immediately returned to the French side. From Thielt, the commissaire d'arrondissement confidentially reported a meeting planned to deliberate on the drawing up of a petition favoring a customs union of Belgium and France, an idea which the commissaire found "excessivement inopportune."[3]

The problem of Belgian workers entering from France was now acute and Rogier read reports recommending that the local gendarmerie be reinforced. Most of these workers had been in France for years, one had been there for twenty-seven years. Many were peaceful and had been the victims of French workers who turned against them, mainly because they were foreign;[4] some British laborers were also victimized.

[1] Gov. (Bruges) to Rogier, Mar. 12, 13, 14, 1848, *ibid*. These include T. E. Sacré (gendarmerie commander in Bruges) to gov., Mar. 12, 1848, and A. Vandenpeereboom to gov., Mar. 11, 1848.

[2] Vandenpeereboom to gov., Mar. 16, 1848 (copy to Rogier on Mar. 18), *ibid*.

[3] Gov. (Bruges) to Rogier, Mar. 15, 16, 17, 1848, *ibid*.

[4] For plight of these Belgian workers and the Prince de Ligne's efforts to aid them, see Ligne to d'Hoffschmidt, Mar. 22 (3 letters), 24, 1848, and Carolus to Materne, Mar. 24, 1848, CNB, I, 237-240, 243-244.

The band, associated in first reports with Grégoire, was of a different sort. Calling itself the Belgian Legion, [1] it had a military organization, was armed, and at Lille awaited reinforcements, according to Hainaut's governor on the 27th. In Lille the expected aid arrived, along with arms from Paris. Belgium's gendarmerie expected imminent attack from the group now rumored at over six thousand, and troops were moved from Bruges to Audenaerde. Warneton or Wervicq seemed likely entry points because of the proximity of the railroad.[2] There were in fact two groups. The first, led by Fosse, entered Quiévrain on March 26 and was readily disbanded by Belgian troops awaiting them at the station. On the 29th, the second group (two thousand strong as it left Paris), also calling itself the Belgian Legion [3] (and often confused with the first group), headed for Brussels via Mouseron, crossing the frontier at Risquons-Tout. They were "rudely received." A force of slightly over two hundred (two companies of the Seventh Regiment) repulsed the invaders who fled in scattered groups. They had been led by Blervacq, and Jaspin, as well as Grégoire, and of these, Jaspin was arrested on the 30th at Roubaix. There remained scattered incidents but, by and large, the Legion disbanded, many fleeing towards Paris, some slipping into Belgium in small groups, and others returning to Lille. Rumors galore circulated. One even held that Louis Napoleon had financed the attack and varying significance was read into the participation of members of the National Guard at Paris as well as students of the Polytechnic School. The goal of the invasion was understood to be the proclamation of a republic in Brussels, accomplished through invasion, burning and pillaging. Jaspin explained the immediate objective to be the death of Leopold. Workers continued crossing the border into Belgium and many, identified as really French, were arrested. Local officials called for reinforcements from Brussels and Ghent as more trouble was expected. Reports were that Grégoire was seen in France recruiting new men on the 30th. The attack at

[1] For diplomatic repercussions of the following incident, see chs. 7 and 8. Diplomatic pouches were filled with mixtures of fact and rumor and reports of the Brussels correspondent for *The Economist* (Apr. 1, 8, 1848) were of the same sort.

[2] Gov. (Bruges) to Rogier, Mar. 22, 23, 27, 29, 1848, including gendarmerie reports, particularly one from Warneton, Mar. 28 at 8 a.m., RP, 74. For able analysis of Belgian workers in northern France, see most of the works cited in ch. 2, footnote 3.

[3] Fosse had recieved aid from Marrast and Parisian municipal authorities while Blervacq's aid came from Caussidière with Ledru-Rollin and Delescluze implicated. See Alvin R. Calman, *Ledru-Rollin and the Second French Republic* (New York, 1922), pp. 92–103 (in Columbia University's *Studies in History, Economics and Public Law*, vol. 103, no. 2). For details on plans to meet and the meeting of the first group, see the report of Auguste Gobert, published in Hymans, *Frère-Orban*, II, 3–8.

Risquons-Tout turned out to be the most prominent case of outright violence regarding Belgium resulting from the revolution in France. In early April, however, there was still apprehension of more such attacks as the southern border of West Flanders was now watched with particular care. Some of the frontier population decided to move to Brussels, joining the flow of still more workers coming peacefully from France.[1]

Meanwhile there were more work stoppages along the frontier area between France and West Flanders. The burgomaster at Menin asked for aid regarding unemployment, particularly from the minister of war.[2] In France, as jobs became scarcer, workers' demands that Belgians be released became stronger and more insistent. In Dunkerque, police said that if Belgians failed to leave, they would not guarantee the safety of anyone's person or property. Between four and five hundred Belgian workers lost their jobs and were forced to leave Dunkerque in early April. Most of these came into Belgium on April 3 in bands of twenty-five or thirty. Behind them they left a scene of local pillaging which French troops made no effort to oppose. In Belgium (largely at Nieuport, Ostend, and Bruges) the newcomers had no hostile disposition regarding the Belgian government; but they added, of course, to the already serious problem of unemployment. There also persisted rumor that the Belgian Legion was reforming near Lille.[3] Though it was learned that the Provisional Government had ordered the arrest of two of the Legion's leaders, there were still prospects of danger with the French officials at Lille suspected of continued complicity. They appeared to be awaiting reinforcements, ten thousand men from Paris. At Warneton with over two hundred unemployed workers, most of them from France, there was an ominous quet; but for the moment they peaceful and honest. On the morning of April 5, another train full of workers from Paris arrived in Bruges and Ghent.[4]

On April 25, the governor reported the death of a French soldier

---

[1] Gov. (Bruges) to Rogier, Mar. 30, 31, Apr. 2, 3, 1848, RP, 74. In the dossier with these are a number of reports which were forwarded to Rogier; of particular interest are: Sacré to gov., Mar. 29, 5 p.m. (account of the Risquons-Tout engagement), 31, Apr. 2, 1848; Vandenpeereboom to gov., Mar. 29, 4: 30 p.m., Mar. 30 (2 letters), 1848; Vandenpeereboom to Rogier, Apr. 2, 1848; H. Carton to gov., Apr. 2, 1848; and Rogier to Chazal, Apr. 2, 1848, forwarding letters from burgomasters of Wervicq and Warneton, both dated Mar. 31, 1848. See also CNB, I, 273; and many entries in DM, V, relate directly to the incident.

[2] Burgomaster at Menin to Haussy, Apr. 3, 1848 (forwarded to Rogier), RP, 74.

[3] Sacré to gov., Apr. 4, 5, 1848; and H. Carton to gov., Apr. 4, 1848, (these forwarded to Rogier), *ibid.* See also Walden to Palmerston, Apr. 4, 1848, F.O. 10/138.

[4] Gov. (Bruges) to Rogier, Apr. 6, 1848, and Sacré to gov., Apr. 8, 1848 (forwarded), RP, 74. For additional evidence on the legion as well as local unemployment, see gov. to Rogier, Apr. 10, 25, 1848, and Sacré to gov., Apr. 19, 20, 1848, *ibid.*

from the garrison at Lille. With a companion he had crossed the frontier near Mouseron and was well within Belgium. After receiving orders to leave from Belgian chausseurs and using insulting language and gestures, he was shot by a chausseur named Mathieu Simon. Simon was arrested, sent to Courtrai, and the governor called the whole episode "very unpleasant." [1]

In France at Marlière near the border, six hundred workers from Tourcoing and Roubaix gathered shouting, "Vive la République!, à bas Léopold! " This prompted the gathering of four hundred Belgians across the frontier, shouting in response, "Vive Léopold!, à bas la République! " Though spirits were high and some rocks thrown by boys of ten and twelve years of age, there was no violation of territory. The bands dispersed and complete order was easily restored after the gendarmerie arrived from Mouseron.[2]

In May there continued to be the problem of more Belgian workers being expelled from France[3] and confidential reports of more danger from the Belgian Legion,[4] but the wave of violence directly stemming from the February Revolution had passed. Harrowing days might yet be ahead; but, on this most dangerous of Belgium's frontiers, mid-May saw the situation uneasy but well in hand.[5]

Compared to the border situation in West Flanders, the effects of France's February Revolution were minor in East Flanders. Despite a natural anxiety over news from Paris, as late as March 13, there was no difficulty whatever. The ad interim governor had been particularly apprehensive over a three day carnival which ended peacefully on the 7th. [6] On the 14th and 15th a few groups pleaded for less work and more money "as in France." Jesuit establishments were menaced but the crowds were easily dispersed by gendarmes with only a few arrests. While there were cries of "Vive la République! " instincts ran more

---

[1] Burgomaster of Echevins to *commissaire d'arrondissement*, Apr. 25, 1848; gov. (Bruges) to Rogier, Apr. 25, 1848, *ibid*. This occasioned a great deal of correspondence; see entries 242–249, 256, 262–268, 274 in DM, V. Annoying episodes such as this, though without loss of life, continued: violence against a 9 year old girl on May 16, propaganda writings in Bruges, and four armed trouble-makers beating on windows and doors singing the "Marseillaise," entering Belgium on the Wervicq road. See gov. to Rogier, May 27, June 17, July 2, 3, 1848, RP, 74.

[2] Gov. (Bruges) to Rogier, Apr. 26, 1848, *ibid*.

[3] Gov. (Bruges) to Rogier, May 2, 1848, *ibid*.; and CNB, II, 8–9, 18–20, 34.

[4] Sacré to gov., May 4, 24, 1848, *ibid*. These letters which were forwarded to Rogier, themselves forwarded two fascinating letters; one from Joseph de Smet, written May 2 in Paris, to the gendarmerie at Courtrai, and the other an unsigned copy of a letter from Paris, May 22, to somebody in Courtrai.

[5] This was Van Praet's view of Belgium as a whole; Van Praet to Van de Weyer, May 17, 1848, VWP, 274.

[6] Ang De Coer to Rogier, Feb. 26, 27, 28, 29, Mar. 5, 6, 7, 13, 1848, RP, 74.

towards pillaging than to any thought-out concrete political goals. The
burgomaster of Ghent decreed the meeting of over five people in a
public place forbidden and cabarets were ordered to be closed by nine
o'clock. The next few days were quiet though trouble was expected at
almost any time – particularly in light of so many outsiders who had
come into the province.[1] A meeting on March 12 of the Electoral
Society was an object of concern for the ad interim governor. Called to
make demands for political and financial reform, the group had little
approval for the suggestion of a customs union with France. Economy
in government services was discussed as well as parliamentary reform.
The diplomatic service, the army, navy, and the judiciary were places
where they felt economies could be instituted and a petition was prepared to this effect to be sent to the chambers in Brussels. Rather
than worrying about a radical committee, the ad interim governor was
relieved at what he called the spirit of "nationality" and government
support.[2] Towards the end of the month there were new crowds but
these were dispersed efficiently. News of repelling the invasion of the
Belgian Legion encouraged officials and made their task easier. A
crowd demonstrated outside the homes of Professors Huet and Moke
at Ghent, because ostensibly these men disapproved the "movement
flamand" which wanted to generalize the use of Flemish to the exclu-
sion of French – highlighting another aspect of the potentialities for disorder facing authorities.[3] There were a few isolated signs of unrest
early in April; but, by and large, disorder was rare and by the 17th
Ang De Coer reported "beaucoup d'ordre" as things were "très tran-
quille." [4] Maintenance of work was really the biggest problem for the
government in East Flanders.

For the government at Brussels the immediate danger seemed to be
largely centered in any efforts at invasion that a resurrected Belgian
Legion might make. They could take comfort in the fact that the armed
invasion had not touched off a general uprising, even in Mariembourg,
surely the most suspect area in Belgium. The threat, however, had
been enough to send Van de Weyer to Palmerston, trying to get an

---

[1] Ang De Coer to Rogier, Mar. 14 (3 letters), 15, 16, 17, 20, 21, 1848, *ibid.*
[2] Ang De Coer to Rogier, Mar. 11, 12, 1848, *ibid.*
[3] Ang De Coer to Rogier, Mar. 28, 29, 30, 31, Apr. 1, 2, 1848, *ibid.* Another letter, also
dated Mar. 31, has a number of reports from subordinates. Huets' difficulties here are only one
aspect of his troubles, involving questions of academic freedom, political interference, foreigners in Belgian universities, socialism, nuances of Catholicism, and the Flemish problem.
Enclosed also is a fascinating 17 page report, Jaegher to Rogier and dated Nov. 9, 1848.
[4] Ang De Coer to Rogier, Apr. 2, 3, 4, 10, 17, 1848, *ibid.*; and Haussy to d'Hoffschmidt,
Apr. 5, 1848, DM, V.

emphatic statement of British support and by April 29, Palmerston had given him numerous assurances that Belgian neutrality and independence was a concern of British policy and that a guarantee by Great Britain was not a "vain word." [1]

---

[1] Van de Weyer to Leopold, Mar. 31, Apr. 12, 15, 29, 1848, VWP, 116.

CHAPTER VII

BELGIAN DIPLOMACY DURING MARCH, 1848

While the problem of formal contact between the French and Belgian governments was being worked out, there was early satisfaction in the absence of large scale rioting. On March 11, Viscount Edmund de Conway called the state of affairs "admirable" and saw no pressing cause for alarm. At the same time he noted that the government was carefully watching the frontiers and the general problem of work stoppages. These two sources of potential danger justified the most careful surveillance.[1]

As the February Revolution encouraged insurrection elsewhere on the continent, the prospects for general European peace and Belgian stability became increasingly dubious. Paul Devaux felt that responsibility for the situation lay solely with France and that events in Vienna and Berlin clearly augmented the chances for war. In such a contingency the French republic could not exist. His only optimism was that two months might pass before the inevitable war.[2]

Insurrectionary movements were scoring momentary triumphs in widely scattered areas as the sense of anarchy and disregard for order reflected actions in Paris. In London the newspapers indulged freely in gross misrepresentation as far as unrest in Belgium was concerned. Van de Weyer complained that any disturbance received a big play with "Revolt" or "Insurrection" being used in large latters to sell papers. He singled out particularly the *London Telegraph* as a case in point, their issue for March 15 carrying "Insurrection at Ghent" for the third time. Among reflective conservatives viewing all this was Louis Napoleon, the Bonapartist pretender then living in London. He was repelled by Ledru–Rollin and wrote that for the interests of France

---

[1] E. Conway to Van de Weyer, Mar. 11, 1848, VWP, 172.

[2] P. Devaux to Rogier, Mar. 24, 1848, RP, 126 (also in Discailles, *Rogier*, III, 245). *The Economist*, Mar. 11, 1848, presents early apprehensions and later confidence; for another voice reporting many adverse criticisms of the Provisional Government, see Greville, *Memoirs* VI, 39–40 (Mar. 14, 1848).

he preferred a hundred times over the old government of Louis Philippe. He found the Provisional Government so abhorrent that he could neither associate with it nor accept the offer he had received of a candidacy in the projected elections. Van de Weyer reported Louis Napoleon's attitude one of "exemplary moderation." [1]

The impact of the February Revolution on Belgian banking circles was immediate. Within a week two banks had closed in Antwerp while in Brussels there were fears that imminent heavy runs might lead to panic. Particular apprehensions centered on the Société Générale and the Banque de Belgique, both holding large Parisian credits. The government moved quickly, introducing a bill to facilitate commercial transactions by authorizing acceptance as legal tender both British Sovereigns and Dutch silver pieces. When another few days passed without events in Paris further disturbing the Belgian economy, the two banks in Antwerp reopened for business.

The government realized fully the sensitivity of financial activities to public confidence. In Brussels the aristocracy was apprehensive of future danger. The lower classes were hurt by a general cancellation of work orders, as reduced spending added to unemployment. D'Hoffschmidt and the British ambassador talked about the necessity of making the upper classes realize that they must continue their orders as a matter of duty. Increased unemployment at just this time was a dangerous prospect and the propertied classes soon came to see the need for continuing and even extending opportunities for employment. The government itself was immersed in the same dilemma. At a time when papers of credit were depreciating and metallic currency was in short supply, the army had to be increased and a number of hasty public works initiated.[2]

The answer to the problem seemed to be a loan from Great Britain and d'Hoffschmidt wrote to Van de Weyer pointing out clearly that the maintenance of stability in Belgium was a great service for Europe and for Britain particularly. It was in the interest of all that Belgium's present sovereignty be maintained since a Belgium either invaded or

---

[1] Van de Weyer to Leopold, Mar. 17, 1848, VWP, 116; and Van de Weyer to d'Hoffschmidt Mar. 16, 1848, CNB, I, 210–214. Louis Napoleon later asked Bates (father-in-law of Van de Weyer) for substantial funds. Bates refused. For interesting analysis of Louis Napoleon, see Van de Weyer to Leopold, June 22, 1848, CNB, II, 118–122.

[2] Walden to Palmerston, Mar. 7, 14 (2), 21, Apr. 4, 1848, and Waller to Palmerston, Mar. 2, 1848, F.O. 10/137. Société Générale problems stemmed from having become a party to Rothschild's loan to the late French government. Both the Société Générale and the Banque de Belgique held paper from the Banque de France, thus linking them closely to the caprices of French finance. See Discailles, *Rogier*, III, 245–253; and *The Economist*, Mar. 25, 1848.

republican would be the signal for a general war. Van de Weyer was instructed to convey these considerations to Palmerston.[1]

In London Van de Weyer's efforts met with sympathy but little success. As Lord Landsdowne outlined the situation to him, it seemed almost as though the British thought their situation was as precarious as the Belgian. Landsdowne made it appear that the ministry simply could not risk a discussion in Parliament of a subject as fraught with implications as a subsidy for Leopold. In addition there was the problem of how to explain in Paris an action that the French would regard as hardly neutral and possibly hostile. Rather than an outright subsidy, Landsdowne, while professing that Britain was impressed by Belgium's stability, wondered whether there might be some "secret manner" Leopold might be aided, some way that would avoid the public "inconveniences" inevitable in a direct open act of the government. Whatever avenue Leopold might finally propose, Landsdowne promised his personal support.[2]

While pressing Landsdowne, Van de Weyer also hoped for aid from other sources. His father-in-law, Mr. Bates, made a number of inquiries of prominent "capitalists in this sort of operation." All rejected as impossible even the smallest loan based on sound guarantees. Complicating Van de Weyer's task was a new financial crisis in Britain. British bankers and investors also had extensive commitments in Paris and were as short of ready cash as their Belgian counter-parts. In order to render any aid to the Belgians, these financiers themselves would have had to borrow. Bates relayed this depressing conclusion to Van de Weyer but continued to make inquiries.[3]

By March 16, Van de Weyer had received a pessimistic letter from Landsdowne. A scheme to get around embarrassing legal difficulties had apparently failed. Landsdowne pointed out the range of British financial problems and concluded with almost a definite refusal. Reporting this, Van de Weyer bitterly and contemptuously blamed the "sordid spirit" of Britain's middle class. More positively he noted that Belgium needed a "financial elan" to complement its political elan and suggested a council of the leading men of all parties and magistracies. Such a group would inspire public confidence which in turn would promote stability.[4]

A week later Lord Landsdowne informed Van de Weyer that the

[1] D'Hoffschmidt to Partoes, Mar. 9, 1848, RP, 83.
[2] Van de Weyer to Leopold, Mar. 6, 1848, VWP, 116
[3] Van de Weyer to Leopold, Mar. 10, 14, 1848, *ibid.*
[4] Van de Weyer to Leopold, Mar, 14, 16, 1848, *ibid.*

cabinet regretted that it simply could not support aid for Belgium in Parliament. Lord Stanley had insisted that any such help must go through Parliament rather than the "condescendance" of Baron Stockmar. One prospect had been the payment of sums due Leopold according to his marriage treaty. However Leopold had voluntarily modified the terms earlier and now legal opinion held that the only way to get funds through this device would be for Parliament to re-establish the original terms of the marriage treaty. The cabinet saw aid only in terms of action by Parliament. This could endanger the life of the ministry since it was agreed that Parliament would consider it as a request to subsidize a foreign sovereign and in this light would surely reject the measure. Van de Weyer's response that a treaty fulfillment was hardly the same as a subsidy drew an agreement from Landsdowne but also the pragmatic observation that it was all embroiled in politics. No matter what the theoretical grounds for the funds were, Parliament would never agree to what looked like an annual subsidy to the King of the Belgians for use in a hostile manner towards the new French republic. The ambassador reported this pessimistic outlook but promised to continue seeking aid in talks with Palmerston, Peel, and others.[1]

With the attack on Risquons-Tout, Van de Weyer approached Palmerston and asked him to use Britain's vast influence in Paris. So far, he felt that the British had avoided offending the Provisional Government and had treated the French with such politeness that they took it for fear. However, now Britain must be more definite. Palmerston briefly tried to defend Normanby's conduct and then gave assurances that Britain would not accept a change of status for Belgium. As for financial aid, his remarks were the same as Van de Weyer had heard from Landsdowne. If it were up to the cabinet, it would be done. However, Commons action would be required and the cabinet was unanimous that this course would be as bad for Leopold as for the ministry itself. Palmerston spoke warmly and with conviction. Van de Weyer's conclusion to Leopold was that all arguments favoring Belgium had been made and that the British ministry would protect its own financial position until there was in Belgium a specific danger that would justify sacrifice.[2]

Thus there was some comfort in this implication of aid if the situation worsened drastically. Leopold was also somewhat encouraged

[1] Van de Weyer to Leopold, Mar. 21, 23, 1848, *ibid*.
[2] Van de Weyer to Leopold, Mar. 31, 1848, *ibid*.

later in March when Belgium's banks appeared "safe," [1] although whether they would survive a number of episodes such as Risquons-Tout was a question. Leopold matched Van de Weyer's efforts to raise money by asking the London *Times* correspondent in Brussels if Great Britain could provide a subsidy to aid in repelling attacks on Belgian territory. In London Van de Weyer was pressing on Delane, the *Times* editor, the idea that Belgium was in a great dilemma. As he put it, the French government was "letting loose these ruffians upon them, affording them all sorts of assistance underhand; and if the Belgian Government repelled them, it was very likely the mob and clubs at Paris would compel the Provisional Government to support them and swallow up Belgium." [2] This was perhaps a deliberate effort to influence the British cabinet through the press after the usual means of persuasion appeared to be failing.

While Leopold and his government were living in anxiety, expecting and fearful of the worst on a day-to-day basis, they received a prelude to the assurances Palmerston finally gave at the end of March. Stratford Canning was departing from London to take up his post at Constantinople. In light of the unrest and violence in Europe, Palmerston decided that he should go by way of Brussels, Hanover, Berlin, Dresden, Vienna, and Munich. At Trieste a steamship was to carry him to Constantinople. He was to meet with resident British diplomats and the respective heads of state, conveying word that British policy was oriented towards the maintenance of peace in Europe. Accompanied by Augustus Loftus, Canning arrived in Brussels on March 19. His specific instructions as far as Leopold was concerned were very general. He was simply to pay his respects and to congratulate Leopold for wise and prudent policies, staying in Brussels as short a time as was compatible with this objective. Anxious to proceed to Berlin, Canning stayed in Brussels only three days. [3]

After talking with Leopold, Canning sent an optimistic report to Palmerston. Leopold and his government, he reported, were following a judicious policy. While they enjoyed cordial relations with both Prussia and Holland, there was a general reliance on the good intentions of the ministry and a strong attachment on the part of the Belgian

---

[1] Leopold to Victoria, Mar. 25, 1848, LV, II, 196–197. See also Walden to Palmerston, Mar. 21, 25, 1848, F. O. 10/137.

[2] Greville, *Memoirs*, VI, 45 (Mar. 31, 1848).

[3] Palmerston to Canning, Mar. 18, 1848, F.O. 30/117 (Canning Mission, Mar. 18–May 13, 1848); and Augustus Loftus, *The Diplomatic Reminiscences of Lord Augustus Loftus, 1837–1862* (2 vols., London, 1892), I, 117.

people for their institutions.[1] For the moment there seemed to be no signs of ill-will from the French government, but the Belgians were quietly preparing for the worst. In all this Leopold seemed as much at ease as his dangerous position could permit. The king was anxious of the future and wanted an agreement about the consequences of a French aggression. He believed that the best safeguard for peace would be the realization that an invasion of Belgium meant a general war. He pressed upon Canning the desirability of a conference in London for such a purpose, noting that extensive British interests were in jeopardy so long as she hesitated in this matter. Leopold also believed changes in the German Diet were required. A more popular representation would improve defense prospects and allay the spirit of discontent and insurrection in Southern Germany. In this he agreed with the King of Prussia. Canning assured Leopold that in any hour of trial Britain could be counted on to fulfill her treaty obligations. At the same time he warned Leopold of premature demonstrations that might encourage the War Party in France, implying that the type of conference Leopold desired might be just such a provocation. From the discussion Canning was assured that the Belgians were successfully following sound policies at home while Leopold received basic assurance of aid in "an hour of trial" but little encouragement for his idea of a general conference.[2]

After talking with Leopold, Canning met with d'Hoffschmidt. The foreign minister had expected some sort of special message from Palmerston but Canning's comments, such as they were, were mainly for Leopold. Canning found that d'Hoffschmidt, while generally agreeing with Leopold's views on additional specific guarantees for Belgium's status of neutrality and independence, was more anxious than the king over the problems of finance and industry. His conversation was particularly dominated by concern for unemployment and for the state of commerce. Though the government had taken steps to raise large sums through forced loans and expected approval from the chambers, the burden would be heavy and the economy would probably suffer, thus increasing the danger. Canning informed Palmerston of all this, though he presumed that Howard de Walden probably had already reported in this vein. He concluded that he was not sure how his observations related to the prospect of some sort of British financial assistance for Belgium in the event of aggression from France.[3]

---

[1] Loftus (*ibid.*) accredited Belgian public stability to Leopold's "wise and judicious rule" and made no mention of the government.

[2] Canning to Palmerston (first report of the Canning Mission), Mar. 21, 1848, F.O. 30/117.

[3] Canning to Palmerston (second report), Mar. 21, 1848, *ibid.*

Belgian relations with Holland during March witnessed a change that was both welcome and long overdue. Immediately after word arrived of the revolution in Paris, the Netherlands government decided to station an army corps near Breda on the Belgian frontier. This decision drew a formal declaration from General Willmar, the Belgian ambassador, that in such a situation the Belgians would be forced to station troops in the border area for observation purposes. This would be in line with the semblance Belgium was trying to create that she was looking to all her defenses and not just those along her southern frontier. While the French border commanded her major attention, to send extra forces to watch the Dutch was to impose an additional burden at a time when she could ill-afford it. The Dutch government cancelled the plan upon consideration of Willmar's protest and the entire episode was over by March 2. Interestingly enough, the French chargé d'affaires in the Hague only learned of it more than a week later on March 10.[1]

At this point d'Hoffschmidt informed Willmar that Belgium was ready to consider any propositions for a defensive alliance that might be made by Holland.[2] An official statement of the Dutch government duplicated the remark of their ambassador in London, Schimmelpenninck, that Holland valued Belgian independence and neutrality and had no intention of profiting from circumstances by attacking Belgium. Further, Holland would not make any joint attack on France with the Northern Powers.[3] British officials in London were pleased by the Belgo-Dutch cooperation. Schimmelpenninck, however, was expecting the worst. He saw a war with France as inevitable. Belgium would become the first battleground and thus should get as many men under arms as possible. Despite Lamartine's reassuring language, the Dutch ambassador pointed out that the leaders in France had always said they wanted the Rhine frontier. To this Van de Weyer replied that Lombardy seemed more menaced than Belgium since an attack on Belgium would provoke British hostility and a coalition of other powers.[4]

---

[1] Breteuil to Lamartine, Mar. 10, 1848, AEF, Pays Bas, 650 (also in DD, I, 138); and d'Hoffschmidt to Chazal, Mar. 2, 1848, DM, V. Van de Weyer to d'Hoffschmidt, Mar. 6, 1848, CNB, I, 123–124, reports that Palmerston condemned the sending of Dutch troops to the Belgian frontier and that the Dutch minister in London, Schimmelpenninck, protested any thought of an armed threat against Belgium. For discussion of cabinet meeting where the basic decision was made to cooperate with Belgium and with Leopold, see Willmar to d'Hoffschmidt, Feb. 29, 1848, ibid., 23–24.

[2] D'Hoffschmidt to Willmar, Mar. 8, 1848, CNB, I, 163.

[3] Willmar to d'Hoffschmidt, Mar. 9, 1848, ibid., 166–167.

[4] Van de Weyer to d'Hoffschmidt, Mar. 8, 1848, ibid., 161–162.

On March 4, an article in *Le Journal de la Haye* appeared which attracted wide attention. It justified increased military preparations by the Dutch government and insisted that these were due to the unsettled state of Europe rather than indications of hostility towards France, though it postulated danger if the moderate voices in Paris were replaced by more extreme ones. It pointed to Belgium's activities since February 24 as an example the Dutch were following and praised King Leopold and his ministers. Further, it insisted that Holland was a loyal friend of Belgium and issued a call for mutual cooperation. A menace towards the security of one was surely a menace to the other and it was essential that each enjoy internal stability and order. Together the two states had prodigious resources unless used against each other; together they could render Europe a great service by preventing an outbreak of general war. The article was impressive and de Breteuil called Lamartine's attention to what he regarded as its friendly tone towards France. The article was copied in the Brussels papers and Britain's ambassador in Brussels sent a copy to Palmerston.[1]

In its wake and contemporaneously with Van de Weyer's lack of success in getting financial support in London, d'Hoffschmidt pressed Willmar to approach the Dutch on the matter of customs reductions. The pressures on Belgian industry were creating sentiment for a union with France and Dutch customs reduction on Belgian cotton products was essential. As d'Hoffschmidt saw it, the Dutch simply could not refuse products of Belgian industry at such a time: employment in Belgium absolutely had to be maintained. Early talks were encouraging as the Dutch spoke of possible ways of accommodating the Belgians while trying to keep the political status quo. However, Willmar was to be disappointed as the Dutch king finally refused economic concessions favorable to Belgium.[2]

In late March Schimmelpenninck was preparing to head the government of Holland. He declared to Van de Weyer that his first act, like Belgium's, would be to increase the army and to put frontiers and forts in a state of defense. He still had little faith in French intentions and feared that Holland and Belgium might be too weak in case of at-

---

[1] Breteuil to Lamartine, Mar. 4, 1848, AEF, Pays Bas, 650. *Journal de la Haye*, Mar. 4, 1848, in IND, I. The particular article can also be found with Walden to Palmerston, Mar. 6, 1848, F.O. 10/137. See *The Economist*, Apr. 29, 1848, for early Dutch apprehensions regarding Belgian stability.

[2] D'Hoffschmidt to Willmar, Mar. 13, 15, 1848, and Willmar to d'Hoffschmidt, Apr. 5, 30, 1848, CNB, I, 199–203, 207–208, 340–342, 393–394. A possibility fruitlessly discussed was a double convention between William as Grand Duke with the King of Belgium and with the King of Prussia.

tack. He unsuccessfully tried to get Van de Weyer to join him in getting assurances from Palmerston of immediate British aid on land and sea. In Van de Weyer's view his actions were both useless and dangerous but in reality they resembled his own earlier precipitant efforts.[1]

The evidence of support for Belgium was a relief in Brussels though there was some hesitation about being too overtly connected with anything that might look like a combination specifically against France. On February 29, the Prince de Ligne had suggested such a union, a separate Belgian, Dutch, British treaty. The Liberal ministry found this idea particularly unpalatable and was more receptive to a general conference of all powers concerned, as urged by Leopold. Thus Belgium welcomed the friendlier relations with Holland, expected to remain close to Britain, but also refused to do anything which might hinder the resumption of normal relations with France.[2]

The crisis resulted in the establishment of direct relations between Leopold and William. Leopold initiated the correspondence, thanking his neighbor for a message of encouragement and support delivered by Baron Bentinck to the Belgian government. William responded with generous assurances in effuse and enthusiastic prose. Interestingly enough the rapprochement hardly included the Belgian cabinet as de Bentinck was treated with confidence only by Van Praet and Leopold.[3]

In Holland the minister of the interior reminded the Chamber that while prudence required certain defensive measures, at all costs these must not be offensive since the early moderation voiced by Lamartine must not be aggravated.[4] In Belgium similar caution prompted Chazal to explain to d'Hoffschmidt that importation of horses by Belgium at this particular instance would be regarded by France as an act of hostility.[5]

---

[1] Van de Weyer to d'Hoffschmidt, Mar. 21, 1848, *ibid.*, 393–394.

[2] Woyna to Metternich, Mar. 5, 1848, with copies of Ligne to d'Hoffschmidt Feb. 29, 1848 (this particular letter also in CNB, I, 26–29), and the rebuff, d'Hoffschmidt to Ligne, Mar. 4, 1848, AEV. A discordant note in the gradual Belgo-Dutch rapprochement was evident in Willmar's report (Feb. 27) that three emissaries had been sent to Belgium hoping for some sort of Orangist uprising in Flanders. On Feb. 29, he mentioned further anti-Belgian intrigues on the part of the king but reported an employee in the royal household as saying that the king lacked energy enough for such designs on Belgium; CNB, I, 9–10, 20–23. While Palmerston sent word to Lamartine on the inviolability of treaties, the British were against an alliance and belligerent action and wanted to avoid irritating France. Also part of the situation was Palmerston's reluctance to take an advance position on a hypothetical development. Thus, while Van de Weyer was sure Britain would come if Belgian neutrality were violated, he recognized that it was not opportune to try to get Palmerston to declare publicly against a republic in Belgium. See Van de Weyer to d'Hoffschmidt, Mar. 11, 16(2), 1848, *ibid.*, 190–191, 210–214, 216–218.

[3] Woyna to Metternich, Mar. 16, 1848, AEV.

[4] Breteuil to Lamartine, Mar. 8, 1848, AEF, Pays Bas, 650.

[5] Chazal to d'Hoffschmidt, Mar. 21, 1848, DM, V.

The French chargé d'affaires at The Hague (de Breteuil) was replaced in March after two years at this post. Before turning things over to his successor (de Lurde), de Breteuil sent Lamartine two extensive confidential accounts,[1] analyzing Dutch society, government, and attitudes as he had come to understand them. He reported that while neither the geography nor the army of the Netherlands would permit it to commit extensive aggression in Europe and despite the obvious Dutch advantages in neutrality, its sovereign might cooperate with policies of the Northern Powers. Dutch foreign policy really was a matter of the king's wishes and de Breteuil felt there were little prospects that the States General might modify the executive power. The provinces were governed, as they had been for centuries, by opulent families with aristocratic ideas. The Prince of Orange followed the politics of his father; and Prince Frederick, though a moderate, was amenable to suggestions from Berlin. Thus, if a war-like measure were strongly encouraged by Prussia and Willmar were disposed to agree, there was no strong opposing element in Holland other than a popular antipathy to soldiering. Prussian influence was strong and in March the Dutch government seemed as much preoccupied with the events of Germany as with those of France. Palmerston had advised them to take a careful and pacific attitude towards the Provisional Government but the Belgian minister at The Hague, General Willmar, suddenly found himself the object of interest and respect. The new state of relations was symbolized by an invitation for Willmar to dine with the Prince and Princess of Orange, an occasion hardly conceivable a few months before.[2]

In early March d'Hoffschmidt informed Leopold that he had been assured that the Provisional Government had no stated aim of forcibly retaking the former frontiers of France. Rather than an armed invasion, Belgium needed to be prepared for a barrage of propaganda in the press and from particular emissaries that might enter the country. In d'Hoffschmidt's view, the guarantees of the powers signatory to the treaties of 1839 were an adequate protection even if the situation worsened.[3] In *l'Eclair* for March 6, 1848, the danger of internal unrest was stated clearly as a message from the Belgian Democratic Association to the Provisional Government made the point that surely Belgium

---

[1] Breteuil to Lamartine, Mar. 10, 15, 1848, AEF, Pays Bas, 650 (also in DD, I, 138–140, 231–233).

[2] Willmar to d'Hoffschmidt, Mar. 16, 1848, CNB, I, 209–210.

[3] [D'Hoffschmidt] to the King (unsigned copy), [In Mar. or Apr., perhaps before Mar. 8, 1848], DM, V.

and other areas bordering France would follow the French example.[1] This was echoed by Ledru-Rollin who spoke of Belgian independence in terms markedly different than Lamartine. He believed that Belgium must be annexed to France but that rather than a French armed invasion, it was a matter of public opinion among the Belgians themselves. The Belgians would adjust their own government structure and having done so, would then have a right to ask the French for protection.[2] The threat of Belgian domestic unrest was acute and the government appropriately recognized it as a major aspect of the problem of independence.

In mid-March Belgian relations with France were superficially on a cordial basis. Sérurier reported a host of dignified visitors who were satisfied with Lamartine's public statements and hopeful that French public life would soon return to a stable pattern. He reported the main concern to be the economic crisis. Lavish balls and parties had largely ceased as the upper classes were reducing their living standard and further aggravating industry.[3]

Meantime d'Hoffschmidt was checking the precise meaning of a *Gazette de Prusse* account that Austria and Prussia were "firmly resolved to repulse with their combined forces every infraction of existing treaties." The Austrian ambassador in London, Dietrichstein, was instructed to ask Palmerston if Britain would be a spectator to an armed violation of the treaties of 1815. A fine point was the distinction between a treaty and a guarantee as discussed by Palmerston. A treaty carried a *right* to intervene in a situation while a guarantee involved a *duty* to intervene.[4]

In checking around, d'Hoffschmidt had received encouraging messages from Berlin and Munich as well as from London and The Hague. Indeed from Bavaria and Prussia the messages were clear that while there was no intent whatever to meddle in French internal affairs, any French aggression would at once find their armies on the march. The candor of the Bavarian assurance to the Belgians surprised Count Woyna whose own position was somewhat embarrassing since d'Hoffschmidt expressed disappointment that Austria had not reacted with

---

[1] Haussy to d'Hoffschmidt, Mar. 8, 1848, *ibid.*

[2] Walden to Palmerston, Mar. 18, 1848, F.O. 10/137. In March the annexation of Belgium became a daily theme for many French socialist journals; see Van de Weyer in Bemmel, *Patria*, II, 344.

[3] Sérurier to Lamartine, Mar. 17, 1848, AEF, Bel., XXX; and also Walden to Palmerston, Mar. 18, 21, 1848, F.O. 10/137.

[4] D'Hoffschmidt to Nothomb, Mar. 17, 1848, AEB, Pr., IX. See also Van de Weyer to d'Hoffschmidt, Mar. 7, 10, 1848, CNB, I, 142–144, 173–175.

a similar encouraging statement.[1] In the background was a fear that Austria might provoke an Italian war into which France would be drawn and the possible consequences were frightening. News of Metternich's fall caused a great sensation in Brussels as elsewhere but it cleared the air temporarily of apprehensions regarding a general war resulting from Austro-Italian policy.[2] Finally, on April 2, Woyna received word that Austria's government congratulated the stability shown by Belgium after the Paris revolution. It was only a lukewarm statement of approval that was hardly a concrete guarantee.[3]

Meanwhile, in March, just after Sérurier had arrived, word came to Brussels of the formation in Paris of the Belgian Legion, a collection of unemployed Belgians, Germans, and other vagabond types. Their avowed aim was to enter Belgium and proclaim the republic. As of March 12, the ministry knew of this group but no news of it had appeared in the journals. The legion's size fluctuated daily but Woyna reported it to be two hundred men at a minimum and probably between three and four hundred. The group left Paris on the 11th, ordered by Lamartine to republicanize Belgium. He piously denied to the Prince de Ligne any connection with the group. He said he had been sounded out for support by plotters against Belgium but had refused to cooperate with them and declared he would resign before having a hand in such an affair. However, his objections did not square with his having signed a decree authorizing formation of a Polish legion of the same sort. Lamartine had also charged Jules Hetzel, a bookseller, with an informal mission to spread republican propaganda in Belgium. Hetzel, along with Tony Johannot, a painter, circulated in Belgium's major cities, associating with the most radical elements. They were carefully watched by the police and their expulsion debated. Sérurier however defended them and in deference to him they were allowed to remain in the country.[4]

The Belgian government was alerted and at the border prepared for the invaders. A few of the group were communists who might have met with some support in Ghent. In Paris Bornstedt was trying to raise

[1] Woyna to Metternich, Mar. 14, 16, 1848, AEV. Woyna suspected that d'Hoffschmidt did not believe he had kept Metternich well posted and that this was the cause of the relative silence from Vienna. He had, however, sent sixteen reports between Feb. 25 and Mar. 16.

[2] Sérurier to Lamartine, Mar. 23, 1848, AEF, Belg., XXX; d'Hoffschmidt to Nothomb, Mar. 19, 1848, AEB, Pr., IX; and O'Sullivan to d'Hoffschmidt, Mar. 21, 1848, CNB, I, 233–235. Ficquelmont, the new foreign minister, had been a friend of O'Sullivan's for 20 years and also knew Leopold well. See also The Economist, Mar. 4, 25, 1848.

[3] Ficquelmont to Woyna, Apr. 2, 1848, AEV.

[4] D'Hoffschmidt to Ligne, Mar. 21, 1848, CNB, I, 235–236.

a whole legion of German communists. However within Belgium the communist threat in 1848 was minor.[1] As the Belgian Legion approached the border, Delescluze, the Commissary-General of the French Provisional Government for the Northern Department notified the Belgian authorities, saying he would cooperate and that the French government disapproved of the legion. Thus Belgian troops were waiting for the legion as its train came into Quiévrain on the morning of March 26. The sight of troops demoralized the legion which had not expected such a reception and it fled in disorder.[2]

In Brussels on the 26th, Sérurier reported talk he had heard. Word was that nine hundred had arrived at Quiévrain and had been efficiently screened. Some were arrested, others allowed to proceed into Belgium to their respective communes, and a number of Frenchmen were sent back to France. Delescluze's contacts with Belgian officials during the episode elicited praise which Sérurier regarded as a good omen for Franco-Belgian relations. Only a day before he had met with Leopold at the monarch's invitation (technically he was not entitled to an audience but Leopold sent word via Van Praet) and Leopold spoke with friendly language towards France and its Provisional Government. On the heels of the Quiévrain episode came news of another convoy of Belgians approaching the border, this group armed and led by four students of the Polytechnic School. Sérurier wrote that he hoped this rumor was false because this time the result would cause a bad effect.[3] In Belgium virtually nobody responded to the distant cries of the legion that Belgians should oust Leopold and establish a republic. The Parisian press generally condemned the Belgian Legion and printed articles demonstrating its "worthless and contemptible character." However this was after the incident on the morning of the 26th and Howard de Walden noted that they should have been as pronounced in their views of the Legion before as after the fiasco.[4]

---

[1] Woyna to Metternich, Mar. 12, 16, 1848, AEV; Walden to Palmerston, Mar. 18, 1848, F.O. 10/137; Bertrand, *Démocratie*, I, 204–207, 449; and Ligne to d'Hoffschmidt, Mar. 11, 1848, CNB, I, 187–189. For Ligne's dealings with these workers, see ch. VI, p. 64, note 4. Specifically see Ligne to d'Hoffschmidt, Mar. 23, 1848, CNB, I, 242–243, and especially Carolus to Materne, Mar. 4, 1848, *ibid.*, 244, where the toll of the disturbances on Ligne's morale and health is noted, and also that the funds at Ligne's disposal are not nearly adequate. D'Hoffschmidt decided to send two men to aid in organizing the repatriation of workers but the efforts and funds were both too small and too late, see d'Hoffschmidt to Ligne, Mar. 25, 1848, *ibid.*, 253–255.

[2] Walden to Palmerston, Mar. 27, 1848, F.O. 10/137; and Woyna to Ficquelmont, Mar. 26, 1848. For details on Delescluze's cooperation and the manner in which plans were made for trains to come into Quievrain, see Hymans, *Frère-Orban*, II, 3–8.

[3] Sérurier to Lamartine, Mar. 26, 1848, AEF, Belg., XXX.

[4] Walden to Palmerston, Mar. 28, 1848 (with press extracts), F.O. 10/137.

On the 29th, the second group crossed the border near Tourcoing and an engagement occurred at Risquons-Tout, a small village near Mouseron. The goodwill just established by Delescluze was now dissipated as the belief spread that French authorities had paid, fed, and armed the invaders after they had arrived from Paris to encamp at Séclin south of Lille. While the Austrian and British ambassadors wrote of Delescluze's complicity as widely accepted, d'Hoffschmidt gave no indication of bitterness or hostility over the event in conversation with Sérurier on the 30th. Sérurier reported that d'Hoffschmidt judged the invasion for what it was (apparently in Sérurier's opinion), the action of poor workers influenced by unscrupulous men. The presence of students from the Polytechnic School and the role of Delescluze suggested connivance of at least part of the Provisional Government despite Lamartine's fine assurances. D'Hoffschmidt, however, did not make such observations to Sérurier. Indeed Sérurier wrote that d'Hoffschmidt was fully convinced that the Provisional Government had not encouraged the ridiculous attack and had praise for the integrity and principles of French foreign policy. For the sake of appearances and particularly to aid the Belgian ministry in its relations with the chambers, d'Hoffschmidt requested that the Provisional Government officially disavow the attack. Sérurier passed this word along to Lamartine, noting that such a disavowal would strengthen the French position in Belgian public opinion as well as create a good effect in the rest of Europe.[1]

The episode at Risquons-Tout heightened existing suspicion of France. From The Hague, de Lurde reported being questioned on the invasion attempts and informed that such affairs were both regrettable and dangerous. The Dutch declared that they trusted the Provisional Government while its foreign minister was Lamartine; but, nevertheless, stability in Holland could not be relied on if Belgium were in revolution.[2]

By the end of March Belgium had survived over a month of danger, discouraged one invasion and repulsed another. It had assurances of support from Holland, Bavaria, Britain, and Prussia if its independence were sorely in danger. Further, it had resumed direct contact

[1] Walden to Palmerston, Mar. 30, 1848, *ibid.*; Woyna to Ficquelmont, Mar. 30, 1848, AEV; Sérurier to Lamartine, Mar. 30, 1848; AEF, Belg., XXX; and d'Hoffschmidt to Nothomb, Mar. 30, 1848, AEB, Pr., IX. The prime suspect was Ledru-Rollin, the French minister of the interior. A careful analysis of his role and that of Delescluze can be found in Calman, *Ledru-Rollin*, pp. 93–103. For an account of these expeditions and their leadership based on court proceedings in Antwerp, see La Gorce, *Seconde République*, I, 182–188.

[2] Lurde to Lamartine, Apr. 1, 1848, AEF, Pays Bas, 650 (also in DD, I, 576–578).

with the French government and was informally on good relations with it. Thus it was pursuing a diplomatic role of strong neutrality as laid down by d'Hoffschmidt on February 28.[1] Internally the problems of economic unrest were receiving careful attention and Leopold and his cabinet were working in close cooperation. With the rest of Western Europe becoming more and more unstable, Belgium stood out as a model of miraculous stability, in the language of Queen Victoria, "a bright star in the midst of dark clouds."[2]

---

[1] D'Hoffschmidt to O'Sullivan, Feb. 28, 1848, IN , I.
[2] Martin, *Consort*, II, 29–30. See also Victoria to Leopold, Apr. 4, 18, 1848, LV, II, 197–198, 203–204.

CHAPTER VIII

APRIL AND MAY, 1848

On the first of April Lamartine replied to the Belgian request that the Provisional Government publish an official article disavowing either direct or indirect participation in the affair at Risquons-Tout. He regarded the charges that the attacks (Quiévrain and Risquons-Tout seen as carried on by the same organization) were well-organized and that Delescluze had played a prominent part as based on hearsay and insisted that such *on dit* information did not merit a serious reply. Further he professed to be amazed at the suspicions of Belgian leaders following the clear and frank talks he had had with the Prince de Ligne.

After disclaiming the need for an explanation, he then provided his own version. Unemployed Belgian workers had indeed asked for assistance "pour reconquérir leur patrie" but the French government had given them neither arms nor munitions. It had given them the means to get home but had not supported any project of hostility against Belgium. He granted that perhaps Delescluze went too far in allowing the rail convoys to proceed to Quiévrain as this had provoked unjust interpretations. A tired and hungry column at Séclin was given food as an act of humanity. They received no arms and nobody knew where their weapons came from. That some Frenchmen were in the group did not make the Provisional Government responsible. Students from the Polytechnic School were there, according to Delescluze, trying merely to protect the security of the French populace. French actions had, indeed, been motivated by a sense of loyalty to Belgium and generosity towards the Belgian workers and were above insinuations to the contrary. Sérurier was to read this message at once to d'Hoffschmidt and Lamartine had already given the Prince de Ligne the same account.[1]

---

[1] Lamartine to Sérurier, Apr. 1, 1848, AEF, Belg., XXX (also in DD, I, 565–567). See the Prince de Ligne's version, *Souvenirs*, pp. 71–73. Interestingly, during the discussion Lamartine noted that the socialist clubs might not like such a public statement of regret. Shortly, the Prince received anonymous letters saying that the clubs had discussed his assassination.

In the Belgian Senate on April 1, d'Hoffschmidt was questioned about the episode. The foreign minister expressed sympathy for the position of the French government and declared his confidence that they viewed Belgium with good-will and clearly could not be made guilty of the attacks. While this was well received in the Senate, the Belgian press strongly criticized the French, particularly Delescluze. There is little doubt that, as Howard de Walden reported, members of the Provisional Government encouraged the expeditions against Belgium but that the Liberal ministry decided to adopt publicly a conciliatory tone. Meanwhile *l'Indépendance* published extensive unofficial accounts of the attacks. A widespread patriotic reaction showed public unity and a moderation of party differences which were more than could probably have been accomplished by any specific initiatives of the government itself.[1]

In the first hours after the attack wild rumors of extensive casualty estimates spread and Woyna was convinced that the Belgian government deliberately wanted to paint the attack in the greatest possible proportions.[2] While the number of gun shots was over five hundred, the dead and wounded numbered nearer thirty than three hundred and the Belgian troops had instilled more fear than harm on their assailants. Woyna had sent to Vienna what he realized by April 1 were exaggerated accounts but he had done this after not only reading the papers but also conversing with Van Praet. He particularly wondered why he had been deliberately misinformed.[3]

The papers in Brussels criticized the French and called for investigations. *L'Indépendance* was as outspoken as the rest and was singled out for special complaint by Sérurier. In language that seemed friendly

In his report to d'Hoffschmidt on April 1, 1848, CNB, I, 296–300, Ligne noted two opinions within the Provisional Government: (1) Ledru-Rollin and others wanting and seeking reunion with Belgium; and (2) those wanting republican forms but also willing to respect nationality. Lamartine was in the second group and was embarrassed by the activities of the first. Ligne had earlier complained to Lamartine of the free convoy made available to the revolutionaries. Lamartine did not deny this but tried to excuse it, saying it was essential to get trouble makers out of Paris but that the French government had not given them arms. He further remarked that the Belgian government had a right to fire on armed invaders. See Ligne to d'Hoffschmidt, Mar. 27, 1848, *ibid.*, 261–262.

[1] Sérurier to Lamartine, Apr. 1, 1848, AEF, Belg., XXX (also in DD, I, 567–568; Walden to Palmerston, Apr. 1, 1848, F.O. 10/138; and d'Hoffschmidt to Ligne, Apr. 2, 1848, CNB, I, 321–323. The arms used were identified as those taken from the Dutch captured in 1832 and deposited since then in the arsenal at Lille.

[2] The information of the Belgian government (and d'Hoffschmidt) regarding events was fairly accurate. See the appropriate Rogier papers in dossier 74 and also d'Hoffschmidt to Ligne, Mar. 30 (2), 1848, and Ligne to d'Hoffschmidt, Mar. 25, 30, 1848, CNB, I, 250–251, 272, 274–285.

[3] Woyna to Ficquelmont, Apr. 1, 1848, AEV.

and sincere, d'Hoffschmidt reaffirmed his hope to see an *official* disavowal in the *Moniteur*. He presented such a statement as essential to curb and dissipate false impressions still rampant in Belgium. At the same time he claimed that it would not compromise the Provisional Government. Indeed, he professed to accept Lamartine's interpretation of events. He sympathized with the difficulties surrounding a new government that was operating without firmly established bases and said that while he would be pleased by a disavowal, he did not want to cause any embarrassment for Lamartine. He claimed the Belgian ministry had never doubted the integrity of the Provisional Government and referred to his own statements of the Senate and similar ones by Rogier to the Chamber.[1]

The *Moniteur belge* for April 4 discussed the Mouseron affair, emphasizing that a host of erroneous reports were circulating and that reliable information was incomplete. The account claimed that many Paris and Lille journals were inaccurate and that the exact source of arms for the legion was unknown, as well as the location where the group camped on its way to the frontier. Sérurier noted that the paper ended without really explaining the affair at all.[2]

At this juncture Lamartine changed his spokesman in Brussels. Sérurier became the secretary of legation serving under Bellocq who was to continue the conduct of unofficial relations until the French Republic was definitely constituted by the National Assembly. Lamartine warned Bellocq of the prejudice and suspicion which abounded regarding France. He wrote that French policy regarding Belgium stressed friendship and mutual respect. Belgium indeed was the state whose institutions most nearly resembled the republican objectives recently sought in France. Lamartine claimed that in following a path of peaceful goodneighborliness towards Belgium, France had abstained from encouraging any idea of the reunion of the two countries. Belgium owed her independence to France and if her people should desire to have a purely republican form of government, this was a matter for free Belgian choice and France had no intention of intervening.[3]

---

[1] Sérurier to Lamartine, Apr. 3, 5, 1848, AEF, Belg., XXX (also in DD, I, 594–595, 640).

[2] Sérurier to Lamartine, Apr. 4, 1848, AEF, Belg., XXX. For best study of Delescluze's role and the complicity of Caussidière and Ledru-Rollin, see Calman, *Ledru-Rollin*, pp. 93–103. Of interest also is La Gorce, *Seconde République*, I, 182–188. That issue of the *Moniteur belge* carried *Moniteur universelle* accounts also. For d'Hoffschmidt's comments on these, see d'Hoffschmidt to Ligne, Apr. 4, 1848, CNB, I, 334–388, and for devastating report proving connivance of French officials, see Hody to d'Hoffschmidt, June 27, 1848, *ibid.*, II, 128–138.

[3] Sérurier to Lamartine, Apr. 9, 1848; Lamartine to d'Hoffschmidt, Apr. 5, 1848; and Lamartine to Bellocq, Apr. 5, 1848, AEF, Belg., XXX (letter to Bellocq also in DD, I, 638–639).

Meanwhile a public disavowal by the French was published in language that d'Hoffschmidt regarded as "a little embarrassing" but satisfactory.[1]

With the political situation drastically being altered with each passing day, especially in Central Europe, d'Hoffschmidt tried to get a firmer commitment of support from Prussia. Of all those signatory to the treaties of 1831 and 1839, he felt Palmerston was the most reassuring. Britain was dependable and had an obligation to aid Belgium. The prospect which d'Hoffschmidt worried about was a direct invasion by France. This, he wrote, was not an inadmissable idea since Lamartine's policy was not that of everyone in France.[2]

Nothomb approached Baron d'Arnim, the Prussian foreign minister, who indicated that he felt d'Hoffschmidt was being too alarmist. Rather than writing and talking of allies for war from an invasion not in sight, he advised sitting tight, keeping order at home and waiting with confidence for the reunion of the French National Assembly. He saw no prospect of a general war. However, he did admit Palmerston's distinction between *right* and *obligation* regarding intervention and judged Belgium to be a case of the latter. Should the French really invade, he said that Prussia, like Britain, would find that its interests would compel intervention to maintain the treaties of 1831 and 1839. Nothomb reported d'Arnim to be sincere but that any part Prussia might play in support of Belgium of necessity would depend on the reconstitution of Prussia and Germany, a two-fold development currently in progress. Ten days later Nothomb wrote that d'Arnim had instructed Bunsen to concert with Palmerston regarding measures to be taken in case of an attack on Belgium by France. Prussia had a host of pressing problems and marked improvement of her position was expected to occur shortly. Meanwhile Belgium must do her best to maintain herself at least until September. At that time there would be no question whatever of immediate, strong, Prussian support. D'Arnim continued to talk of France as peacefully motivated. Van de Weyer noted that Prussia's language in London was different than it was in Berlin. Bunsen asked Palmerston if Prussia could depend on British cooperation in case Belgian neutrality had to be defended. As

---

[1] D'Hoffschmidt to Nothomb, Apr. 4, 1848, AEB, Pr., IX.

[2] D'Hoffschmidt to Nothomb, Apr. 11, 1848, *ibid.*; and Van de Weyer to d'Hoffschmidt, Mar. 27, 31, Apr. 5, 1848, CNB, I, 259–260, 286–288, 343–348.

d'Hoffschmidt expected, Palmerston responded explicitly in the affirmative.[1]

Among "reconstitutions" taking place in Europe in 1848 was the temporary establishment of provisional governments in Venice and Milan. D'Hoffschmidt wondered what Belgium's attitude should be if they accredited their agents to both Paris and Brussels, a fairly common procedure. He felt that Belgium had a right to refuse even officieuse relations with these governments and argued that they were provisional in a different sense than the French government. In the French case all other authority had disappeared while in Italy there was still insurrection. The Emperor had not abdicated (as Louis Philippe had) and his armies were still south of the Alps. Though he was convinced Belgium had the right to refuse, at the same time he expected that Sardinia, Naples, Rome, Tuscany, and France would all accept the Lombard representatives. What would be the public and international reaction to a different action by Belgium, or would there be any at all? He presumed that Prussia might have the same problem and instructed Nothomb to probe d'Arnim on the subject.[2]

D'Arnim's response was an emphatic "No" – not only in terms of Prussia's accepting such a delegation but also on the propriety of Belgium doing so. He reminded Nothomb that while there was such a thing as a French nation, there was no Venetian or Lombard nation and if a real crisis developed, it would be a matter of general concern for the European powers. Revolution in Italy could have no analogy whatever to the February Revolution because of the dynastic aspect of the situation in France. Further he reminded Nothomb that from a Prussian perspective, Austria was a fellow German power as well as one of the five guaranteeing Belgian independence.[3]

In the area of diplomatic representation a touchy problem was finally solved when the Pope agreed to the appointment of Leclercq. Leclercq's moderate liberalism was far less pronounced than Roman liberal views and continued Papal opposition made little sense. The appointment now was accepted in flattering language for Leclercq and the Belgian cabinet, with neither conditions nor reservations. No grudges were held and, in retrospect, Van de Weyer concluded that

---

[1] Nothomb to d'Hoffschmidt, Apr. 17, 27, 1848, and d'Hoffschmidt to Nothomb, May 2, 1848, AEB, Pr., IX; and Van de Weyer to Leopold, Apr. 29, 1848, VWP, 116. While speculating about Changarnier being named French ambassador in Berlin, Arnim expressed complete satisfaction with Circourt and the manner in which he had represented the French government. See Westmorland to Palmerston, Apr. 21, 25, 1848, F.O. 64/286.

[2] D'Hoffschmidt to Nothomb, Apr. 6, 1848, AEB, Pr., IX.

[3] Nothomb to d'Hoffschmidt, May 15, 1848, *ibid.*

the objection by Rome had really been a matter of testing the leanings of the Liberal Ministry.[1]

As Belgian diplomatic representation in Rome was being regularized, friction developed between d'Hoffschmidt and Van de Weyer. On April 6, d'Hoffschmidt wrote to Van de Weyer reprimanding him for publicity about his visits to the Count de Neuilly (Louis Philippe) and others of the Orleans family, and for being received by the Prince of Prussia. D'Hoffschmidt claimed these reports were ill-received in Belgium and he dreaded an impending interrogation in the Chamber. He went on to insist that Van de Weyer use more circumspection and prudence.[2]

Van de Weyer informed Leopold that this message was "si blessante" that he had decided to request a replacement.[3] To d'Hoffschmidt he vigorously denied that this actions had been inappropriate. He claimed that he had read all the British journals and had found only one mention of his visits to Claremont. Besides, he had only been there twice to deliver letters and packages from Brussels which had been sent via his office – and he had made no visits at all to other members of Louis Philippe's family. Indeed, he insisted he was more circumspect than most of his colleagues who, without the motives he had, went every week to Claremont. As for the Prince of Prussia, he was no fugitive, Albert had received him and there was nothing wrong with being received by him in turn. Furthermore, the Prince of Prussia had received the whole diplomatic corps. Palmerston was visiting the Prince when Van de Weyer went to inform him of Risquons-Tout and this was the special audience. He testily concluded that he had served Belgium since 1828 and would not accept from anyone the blame d'Hoffschmidt had sent in his direction – therefore, d'Hoffschmidt should send to London a man he felt could serve Belgium better.[4]

Before d'Hoffschmidt had received this message, he sent off to Van de Weyer a note implying more criticism. Van de Weyer's opinions on

---

[1] Nothomb to d'Hoffschmidt, Apr. 8, 1848, *ibid.*; Walden to Palmerston, Apr. 8, 1848, F.O. 10/138; Woyna to Ficquelmont, Apr. 8, 1848, AEV; and Van de Weyer in Bemel, *Patria*, II, 345. Leclercq accompanied the Pope to Gäete but was shortly replaced by the Prince de Ligne (*Souvenirs*, pp. 87–124). The Ligne appointment created new friction. Because he was accredited to other Italian courts as well as Rome, the rank of the Papal representative in Brussels needed to be reduced. Also, in Sardinia there was marked concern over the presence in the Austrian army of the son of the Prince de Ligne. See Walden to Palmerston, Oct. 9, Nov. 4, 1848, F.O. 10/139; and Quinette to Drouyn de Lhuys, Dec. 22, 1848, AEF, Belg., XXX.

[2] D'Hoffschmidt to Van de Weyer, Apr. 6, 1848, CNB, I, 351–352.

[3] Van de Weyer to Leopold, Apr. 8, 1848, VWP, 116.

[4] Van de Weyer to d'Hoffschmidt, Apr. 8, 1848, CNB, I, 354–356.

British support, if Belgium were in serious danger, were reassuring but actually only conjectures. He really could get a more definite view from Palmerston without a precise question. The next day he replied to Van de Weyer's offer to resign. He claimed Van de Weyer exaggerated the substance of his letter of the 6th. (Van de Weyer had not exaggerated at all.) He, as foreign minister, had the right to make observations and this was all he had done. He reemphasized that reports were embarrassing and that they had been discussed in a cabinet meeting with Leopold presiding. Magnanimously he said he would pass over in silence the last of Van de Weyer's letter, the portion dealing with the idea of resignation.[1]

Van de Weyer was not to be so easily put off. He believed the charges against him originated in an irresponsible Belgian press and if the government chose to believe them, he could not in honor continue as his country's agent on London. D'Hoffschmidt replied that there was no parliamentary reason at all for Van de Weyer to resign. He praised him and told him he was held in high regard and that Belgian journals had also attacked cabinet officials in strong language. He ended with an eloquent plea to continue through the difficult period.[2] This was the end of the episode and no hint of friction or ill-will appears in later messages.

Among the myriad of problems concerning d'Hoffschmidt in April was the dangerous situation in the Grand Duchy of Luxemburg. The foreign minister saw the whole problem there as basically concerning trade and tariffs. The whole problem would be solved with free trade between the two parts of the former Luxemburg and this could be arranged only by a customs association between Belgium and the Grand Duchy. The accession of the Duchy to the Zollverein made this impossible. The solution, he believed, was to have the Zollverein moved back to the Prussian border so that the Duchy were not included. He wrote to Nothomb, asking that d'Arnim be approached with this suggestion. The misfortune in Luxemburg (duchy) had been caused by the separation of 1839 and the situation was dangerous. A modest commerce at points along the frontier already indicated the advantages which could come if free trade arrangements could be made between Belgium and the Grand Duchy. D'Hoffschmidt even went so far as to suggest that such an agreement was indispensable for

[1] D'Hoffschmidt to Van de Weyer, Apr. 10, 11, 1848, *ibid.*, 361–363, 366–369.

[2] Van de Weyer to d'Hoffschmidt, Apr. 15 (or 16), 1848, and d'Hoffschmidt to Van de Weyer, Apr. 25, 1848, *ibid.*, 372–374, 384.

the mere maintenance of the then very shaky political status quo.[1]

The response of Prussia's foreign minister to this message was a forthright statement that any arrangement where the Grand Duchy would leave the Zollverein would not be tolerated by Prussia and Germany. He thought that probably on some items Belgium and the Grand Duchy could make some agreements but Luxemburg must stay in the Zollverein. He suggested that Belgium should make a zollverein with Holland which, after a French refusal to join, would lead to entry into the German Zollverein.[2]

D'Hoffschmidt replied that Nothomb should again press the point that tariff barriers between the two Luxemburgs must be lowered drastically. As for d'Arnim's view that some agreements were possible, d'Hoffschmidt contended that all that could be done had been done in the treaties of June 1839 and September 1844. The idea of a customs union between Belgium and Holland, he wrote, was not a practical idea for the present. D'Arnim proved no more receptive than before. He urged that particular provisions be carefully examined before declaring, as d'Hoffschmidt's dispatch had, that the former treaties eliminated all hope of progress in this direction. Partial arrangements indeed held many possibilities. He maintained his former position that for the Grand Duchy to leave the Zollverein was out of the question, an act that Prussia and Germany "would not be able to tolerate." [3]

The Belgian government had proposed the idea of a commercial union between Belgium and Holland. This was well-received in Belgium and hopes were high that one could be negotiated. However, the Dutch rejected the proposal, showing that it was not so simple to coordinate Belgian and Dutch interests. Dutch commerce was a sprawling affair and poor trade conditions in its colonial commerce was an important factor in their refusal.[4]

Early April in Belgium brought rumors of another attack being planned by the Belgian Legion. This time the numbers of the attackers were expected to be much larger and a portion of the

---

[1] D'Hoffschmidt to Nothomb, Apr. 2, 1848, AEB, Pr., IX. On Apr. 2, d'Hoffschmidt asked Willmar (CNB, I, 317–320) to check on the possibilities of Luxemburg leaving the Zollverein for a customs union with Belgium. Willmar replied on Apr. 9 (*ibid.*, 359–360) that as far as a custom arrangement with Luxemburg was concerned, it was to Prussia rather than Holland that Belgium should address her views.

[2] Nothomb to d'Hoffschmidt, Apr. 27, 1848, AEB, Pr., IX.

[3] D'Hoffschmidt to Nothomb, May 5, 1848, and Nothomb to d'Hoffschmidt, May 8, 1848, *ibid.*

[4] Haussy to d'Hoffschmidt, Apr. 5, 1848, DM, V; Lurde to Lamartine, Apr. 23, 1848, AEF, Pays Bas, 650 (also in DD, I, 997–998); and Willmar to d'Hoffschmidt, Apr. 5, 30, 1848, CNB, I, 340–342, 393–394.

Brussels garrison was sent to Mons where it could move readily to a threatened point on the frontier. At the same time it would insure more stability in the mining area where some miners had been forced to stay out of the mines and make common cause with other workers. The next attack never came but the threat was omnipresent. Ledru-Rollin was rumored to be organizing more armed bands which would be the avant-garde of an army of invasion. Van de Weyer wrote that the French demagogue was waiting only for a serious problem, such as an insurrection in Ireland, to distract the British. On the other hand the Irish were waiting for Britain to be involved elsewhere. In this precarious situation the cabinet policy was peace if at all possible. An outright conquest of Belgium by France would jolt Britain from her position but her statesmen believed such an event could not occur without an internal movement in Belgium. Thus they favored the maintenance of order in Belgium; stability in Belgium was as vital to them as stability in Ireland and the two problems were connected.[1]

Woyna believed that the Provisional Government was underhandedly promoting schemes to republicanize Belgium and suggested to his government that, considering the strong interests in Britain for peace, it was quite possible that Britain would go along with the idea of a republican Belgium providing its borders were unchanged. A republican Belgium beside a republican France would really not be inimical to British security and it would take a French army entering Belgium outright to get a large majority in Britain to favor war. King Leopold had no illusions about British politics. By now he had completely recovered his nerve and he spoke energetically and professed a deep faith in an exceptional destiny for the Belgian monarchy. In Brussels many thousands cheered him on the occasion of a military review on the birthday of his son, the Duke of Brabant. Such spontaneous public warmth was unusual for Belgians and undoubtedly cheered the king as well as his cabinet.[2]

In diplomatic circles in Berlin the attacks on Belgium's frontier had created a sensation and general sympathy for Belgium's position. Nothomb kept d'Arnim as well-informed as he could and in turn d'Arnim discussed the matter with de Circourt, the envoy of the French Provisional Government. He pointed out the dangers of such attacks and asked what the role of the French government would be

[1] Van de Weyer to Leopold, Apr. 15, 1848, VWP, 116.
[2] Walden to Palmerston, Apr. 4, 11, 1848, F. O. 10/138; and Woyna to Ficquelmont, Apr. 8, 10, 1848, AEV.

if by surprise the Belgian republic were proclaimed in a small town on the frontier. While de Circourt vigorously denounced the raids, Prussia had made clear its concern for Belgian independence.[1]

In London Palmerston carefully weighed reports of the hostile bands on Belgium's frontier and publicly recalled the guarantees made to Belgium by the four powers. He reassured Van de Weyer and promised close cooperation in Paris; Normanby would communicate to the Prince de Ligne all reports that might be of interest to the Belgian government.[2] However a month later Normanby was leaving his post in Paris and the Prince de Ligne had asked for a leave though Van Praet indicated that he would be encouraged to remain in Paris.[3]

Bellocq arrived in Brussels on April 10, 1848. His first conversation with d'Hoffschmidt amounted to the exchange of sentiments of goodwill and friendship. Bellocq had been named as an Envoy Extraordinary and Minister Plenipotentiary even though he was to conduct only unofficial relations. This made a favorable impression on the Belgians who were also pleased with Bellocq personally. He had been secretary of legation at Brussels in 1830 and for many years was the French minister at Florence. Politically he was regarded as an extreme moderate, perhaps even legitimist, and as an objective observer was expected to counteract the strong feeling and misrepresentation of Belgium that came to Paris from the public press and authorities in Northern France. Bellocq was received by Leopold but without the usual formality due a new minister. In the hour-long discussion the king commented that although relations were informal, nevertheless Bellocq's mission itself had an official character. Leopold spoke in much more detail than d'Hoffschmidt had about Mouseron, concluding that after a revolution there were naturally many problems and that France would find Belgium not only an inoffensive neighbor but an affectionate one. Bellocq reported all this to Lamartine who wrote with relief that mutual goodwill appeared reestablished and perhaps the question of the workers had ended. D'Hoffschmidt confided his satisfaction over Bellocq's appointment to Woyna and showed Austria's envoy a dispatch from the Prince de Ligne as well. Woyna forwarded a copy to Vienna since he suspected that Lamartine would say things

---

[1] Nothomb to d'Hoffschmidt, Apr. 6, 1848, AEB, Pr., IX.

[2] Van de Weyer to Leopold, Apr. 12, 1848, VWP, 116.

[3] Van Praet to Van de Weyer, May 6, 1848, VWP, 274. The Prince de Ligne had been instructed against taking a leave as early as March 6. See d'Hoffschmidt to Ligne, Mar. 6, 1848, CNB, I, 131–132.

to the Prince de Ligne that he might not tell the Austrian representative then in Paris, M. de Thom.[1]

By mid-month concern over border violations subsided somewhat although Delescluze gave signs of hostility towards Belgium. In planting a tree of liberty near the frontier he remarked that soon its roots might spread under the frontier and topple the monument at Waterloo. However other signs were encouraging. The paralysis of business caused earlier by the suspension of credits was declining as government action was proving effective. Also prices of bread, meat and other essentials were dropping and the prospect was bright at this point for a year of good crops.[2] The shooting on the 24th of a French soldier near Mouseron was an isolated incident which Belgian officials regretted and d'Hoffschmidt gave assurances to Bellocq that the soldier responsible would be tried and punished as though the man killed had been a Belgian.[3] Meanwhile, Belgian papers spread rumors of a French army forming near the Belgian frontier. Lamartine and the Prince de Ligne discussed the matter and the foreign minister's remarks indicating that the reports were largely false satisfied d'Hoffschmidt. Lamartine explained that a corps of forty thousand men on the frontier near Belgium had been decided on by the French government but simply as a matter of planning; the force was designated only on paper, merely to satisfy public opinion in France.[4]

On April 22, 1848, Bellocq wrote to Lamartine an interesting analysis of the prospects of republicanism in Belgium. The Belgians, he reported, did not seem to want a republic. They saw the revolution in France with some admiration but without enthousiasm. They were proud of having preceded the French in peaceful attainment of liberties. The king was really a president with a magnified title in recognition of service he had rendered by accepting leadership at a time of emergency. Rather than resenting his position, the recent events in Europe and the armed attack had enhanced his standing in the public mind.

[1] Bellocq to Lamartine, Apr. 11, 13, 17, 1848, and Lamartine to Bellocq, Apr. 17, 1848, AEF, Belg., XXX (all also in DD, I, 771, 808–810, 864–866); Walden to Palmerston, Apr. 15, 1848, F.O. 10/138; and Woyna to Ficquelmont, Apr. 10, 1848, AEV.

[2] Walden to Palmerston, Apr. 18, 1848, F.O. 10/138. Within Belgium there was divided sentiment over allowing the Waterloo monument to remain. D'Hoffschmidt argued against its destruction, pointing out that Belgians fought bravely on both sides and to destroy it simply because France had become republican made no sense, especially since it had stood for thirty years and had not been destroyed during the two initial French invasions of Belgium. See d'Hoffschmidt to Rogier, May 7, 1848, RP, 126.

[3] Bellocq to Lamartine, Apr. 26, 1848, AEF, Belg., XXX (also in DD, I, 1034–35).

[4] D'Hoffschmidt to Nothomb, May 2, 1848, AEB, Pr., IX; and d'Hoffschmidt to Ligne, Apr. 18, 1848, and Ligne to d'Hoffschmidt, Apr. 21, 26, 1848, CNB, I, 377–381, 385–386.

There was in Belgium no segment of the population of any importance that actively desired a republic. The rich and noble classes excited no hostility on the part of the poor and working classes because in the past they had helped the poor, they had been good proprietors and were well-regarded. Rather than an effective republican party, there were only a few scattered republicans in Belgium. A widespread conviction held that a republican Belgium could not live independently and that it would be absorbed inevitably by France. Bellocq reported this sentiment to be so strong that even men favoring radical changes advocated caution and a prudent waiting for the outcome of events in France. In this situation Bellocq concluded that anything promoting a republic in Belgium would ultimatley be bad for both France and Belgium. A Belgian republic would lead France into war with Britain and there would be other enemies as well. Further, reunion of France and Belgium would create rivalries and discord among French industries in Northern France. All this, he remarked, was hypothetical because he realized that his government respected nationalities and, after all, the Belgian ministry was sincere in its goodwill towards France.[1]

By early May, though the economy was improving, the Belgian government's need for funds was still acute. The treasury was ill-prepared for an extended period of crisis and the search for foreign loans continued. D'Hoffschmidt even considered Nicholas of Russia as a prospect. He wrote to Nothomb asking if it would be feasible to present the question to Meyendorff. He cautioned that it was essential that Belgium not appear in the position of being subsidized by an autocrat. However Russia had appreciated Belgian firmness since February and might possibly help with a loan. Should he meet with Meyendorff, Nothomb was to be sure the conversation was completely void of any appearance of being official since, as he noted, the question was extremely delicate.[2] Belgium was ready and willing to have regular diplomatic relations with Russia but was unable to take the initiative since, as d'Hoffschmidt pointed out, an exchange of agents would credit the rumors of a coalition against France that French papers, especially the *National*, were spreading. Nonetheless Nicholas was reported by Van de Weyer as intending shortly to propose normal diplomatic relations.[3]

---

[1] Bellocq to Lamartine, Apr. 22, 1848, AEF, Belg., XXX (also in DD, I, 962–963).

[2] D'Hoffschmidt to Nothomb, May 5, 1848, AEB, Pr., IX (also in CNB, II, 16–17). On June 20, d'Hoffschmidt definitely instructed Nothomb (CNB, II, 113–114) to let the idea drop unless the situation changed.

[3] Van de Weyer to d'Hoffschmidt, May 11, 1848, and d'Hoffschmidt to Van de Weyer, May 22, 1848, CNB, II, 28, 59–60.

Nothomb's interesting reply was predictably negative. He did not go into the obvious unlikelihood of Nicholas lending aid to a state that so far he had steadfastly refused to recognize. Rather, he pointed to a number of large projects which Nicholas was pushing to completion and which he hoped would be finished by 1856. There was also for Nicholas the cost of a large army, an expense which had been increased since February. After considering Russian finances, Nothomb said he would see Meyendorff if d'Hoffschmidt still desired it but personally he believed "that financially there was nothing to hope for" in this direction. When d'Hoffschmidt read this letter, he penciled a large "Non!" in the margin and the idea was dropped.[1]

The financial problem still existed. The saving grace was that general trade was maintained at an unusually high level considering that the period was one of widespread insurrection in Europe. Thus government revenues remained generally high, indeed, up half a million francs over the first three months of 1847. Aid on a stop-gap basis was continued to the Société Générale which was suffering the joint indignity of being a public scandal and of having its records publicly debated for the first time. In addition to holding too much paper from the Banque de France, it also had lent extensively to commercial companies that were not solvent.[2]

Border violations along the Belgian-French frontier were of most concern but in early May forty or fifty armed soldiers from the garrison at Malmedy entered Belgium briefly. It was a fleeting episode of no lasting consequence but d'Hoffschmidt felt compelled to lodge complaints with the Prussian minister at Brussels. It was, as he put it, a territorial invasion by armed might and a very grave matter. He asked for an explanation and that steps be taken preventing such an incursion again. Seckendorff transmitted the complaint and assured d'Hoffschmidt that a satisfactory response would soon be given.[3]

In early May Count d'Apponyi stopped in Brussels to see Woyna on his way from Paris to a vacation in Hungary. He reported the proletariat in control in Paris with only those legitimists in the National Assembly who were now willing supporters of republican policies. At the same time he believed in the ultimate restoraton of a monarchy and probably some sort of Orleanist regency. To Woyna this seemed contra-

[1] Nothomb to d'Hoffschmidt, May 13, 1848, AEB, Pr., IX (also in CNB, II, 31–32).
[2] *The Economist,* Apr. 29, May 6, 13, 20, 1848.
[3] D'Hoffschmidt to Nothomb, May 13, 1848, AEB, Pr., IX.

dictory. D'Apponyi saw Lamartine as moving with no compunction from one position to another.[1]

D'Hoffschmidt regarded the recent elections in France as assuring a wise majority and foreshadowing Lamartine's nomination as President of the Republic. The Belgian minister estimated also that the prospects of internal order in France were enhanced and the dangers of war for Belgium were correspondingly decreased. In this situation there was no need for additional French declarations of peaceful intent and Belgians could face the future with some measure of confidence.[2]

This was also the general view of Howard de Walden. He saw Belgian prospects as not only satisfactory but even cheering compared with the rest of Europe. Though a potato disease was to create a "great and general calamity" on all low ground in the area from Ostend to Cologne by mid-August, in early May the prospects were for a "magnificent harvest." He reported domestic calm throughout Belgium and managed to see a good side to irritating and insulting border friction on the frontier facing France. These kept the populace disturbed against republicans and against France. Trade was still sluggish but credit was slowly reviving as everyone realized the danger and the upper classes made sacrifices to enable the poor to earn a livelihood. The government was well-supported and Leopold was popular.[3]

A week after this optimistic report, however, the British ambassador was much soberer, relaying word that a member of the French government had spoken frankly of a foreign policy for the republic which repudiated the obligations of the treaties of Vienna and looked ahead for the reestablishment between France and Belgium of the frontier as it was in 1814; this meant a reannexation to France of the eight cantons of Dour, Merbes le Chateau, Beaumont, Chimay, Valcour, Florennes, Beauraing, and Gedinne.[4] There was further apprehension from a diplomatic report to the National Assembly by Lamartine where Belgium was hardly mentioned and the Rhine implied as the frontier. The Prince de Ligne was instructed to complain and especially

---

[1] Woyna to Ficquelmont, May 5, 1848, AEV. See also Ligne, *Souvenirs*, p. 68.
[2] D'Hoffschmidt to Nothomb, May 2, 1848, AEB, Pr., IX.
[3] Walden to Palmerston, May 9, Aug. 17, 1848, F.O. 10/138.
[4] Walden to Palmerston, May 16, 1848, *ibid*. As a matter of fact, there were new efforts and revived plans for an invasion by the Belgian Legion. The Belgian government, however, received confidential reports from inside the Legion and was prepared for the invasion which, as it worked out, failed to take place. See copies of letters written (by J. de Smet on May 2 and 22, 1848) from Paris to Sacré, gendarmerie commandant at Bruges, RP, 74. Lamartine had earlier noted to Ligne that if he were forced out as foreign minister, the problem of invading bands would be much worse; Ligne to d'Hoffschmidt, Apr. 8, 1848, CNB, I, 356–358.

to regret no mention of Belgian independence and friendship for France. Bastide told Ligne that nothing unfavorable was intended but Ligne agreed with d'Hoffschmidt that the omen was unfavorable.[1]

At the same time a secret meeting occurred in the offices of the *National* in Paris. A number of Belgian republicans attended. The paper's editors felt that the new republic would fall if a peaceful foreign policy was continued. Unemployed workers were a distinct menace and the only answer was some sort of dramatic diversion. The main editor recommended the conquest of Belgium with the proclamation of a Belgian republic and it was estimated that two months would be necessary for a major attempt to unify the futures of France and Belgium. Word of this meeting leaked out and Van de Weyer recommended redoubled precautions at Brussels, Ghent, and Charleroi.[2]

Hostility to Belgium in the editioral offices of the *National* was clear on March 20 when the paper carried an article which, among other things, suggested that Belgium, with Holland and Britain, had offensive plans against France. At a time when relations were generally improving, this article disappointed d'Hoffschmidt who at once instructed the Prince de Ligne to discuss the matter with Jules Bastide, Lamartine's successor in the foreign ministry. On the 22nd, *l'Indépendance* in Brussels ran a refutation of the article. Bastide's attitude was simply to point out that the *Nationel* was not an official paper and to make light of the episode. At the same time he noted that the defandant who was tried for murdering a French soldier had been acquitted by the tribunal at Bruges to the applause of the population. This created resentment in France and Bastide instructed Bellocq to ask the Belgian government for the basic documents of the tribunal's procedure.[3]

Simultaneously over much of Western Europe a wave of republican intrigues was touched off or inspired by agents from France and Van de Weyer traced this to the meeting at the *National* office. For the

[1] D'Hoffschmidt to Ligne, May 10, 1848, and Ligne to d'Hoffschmidt, May 13, 1848, CNB, II 26–28, 32–34.

[2] Van de Weyer to Leopold, May 22, 1848, VWP, 116. Over a month before, d'Hoffschmidt was complaining about the *National* and also Bastide's connection with it; Bastide, then secretary general in the foreign ministry, denied complicity. See d'Hoffschmidt to Ligne, Apr. 12, 1848, and Ligne to d'Hoffschmidt, Apr. 15, 1848, CNB, I, 370–372.

[3] Bellocq to Bastide, May 22, 1848, and Bastide to Bellocq, May 29, 1848, AEF, Belg., XXX (also in DD, II, 396, 536). The article was also disturbing to the British. See Tallenay to Bastide, June 8, 1848, DD, II, 741. The request for details and documents on the judgment first was unsuccessfully addressed to the Prince de Ligne by Ledru-Rollin, on the initiative of Arago; Ligne, *Souvenirs*, p. 79. At this time the Prince of Prussia, returning from London, was talked into passing swiftly through Belgium, to avoid arousing French suspicions. See d'Hoffschmidt to Van de Weyer, May 16, 18, 19, 1848, CNB, II, 40–41, 45–47, 49.

moment, friction with Belgium seemed only part of an over-all policy of promoting general unrest in Europe.[1]

After Bastide's appointment as foreign minister following Lamartine, the Belgian government regarded the French Republic as definitively founded and wished to be the first to recognize it officially, ahead of all the other European powers. On May 20 Bellocq wrote to Bastide of this Belgian interest, noting that it was also the attitude of Leopold as well as the Rogier cabinet. Van de Weyer had kept Palmerston informed of these intentions and the British minister voiced no objection. D'Hoffschmidt, Bellocq believed, was particularly impatient to get the matter of official double diplomatic representation settled. The Belgian minister said on the 19th at a soirée that he had decided to instruct the Prince de Ligne to approach Bastide on the matter.[2]

After receiving appropriate letters on the 28th, Bellocq presented his credentials to King Leopold and the act was accomplished. Almost at once and to his surprise and pleasure, he received an invitation to dine with Howard de Walden to celebrate Queen Victoria's birthday but minor uniform details prevented his acceptance. The British ambassador judged him a good man and a replacement of Rumigny that would be regretted only by some political priests, Jesuits, and the intolerant of the Catholic Party. Letters accrediting the Prince de Ligne were sent out on the 28th.[3]

D'Hoffschmidt was pleased with the symbol of more appropriate relations with France and talked freely to Bellocq. Warming expansively to the new relationship, he told Bellocq that shortly after the February Revolution some propositions had been made to Belgium by several powers, including Russia, Prussia, Holland and even Austria, that they recognize the existence of the Republic only after the French National Assembly had drawn up a constitution. However, d'Hoffschmidt went on, Belgium had declared openly and loyally

[1] Van de Weyer to Leopold, May 26, 1848, VWP, 116. Lamartine's career was passing its apex. A critic observed that he had "imagined that he could conciliate all the parties, and he was made the fool of each of them... considered under Louis Philippe's reign a political simpleton, and his conduct since February last proves that he was well judged." *The Economist*, Aug. 26, 1848.

[2] Bellocq to Bastide, May 20, 1848, AEF, Belg., XXX; and Tallenay to Bastide, May 18, 1848, DD, II, 305 (Bellocq's letter also in DD, II, 361–362). The Prince de Ligne found Bastide friendly, democratic, moderate and of the opinion that marriages of princes constituted national treaties; Ligne, *Souvenirs*, pp. 79–81.

[3] Walden to Palmerston, May 16, 1848, F.O. 10/138; Bellocq to Bastide, May 28, 29, 1848, AEF, Belg., XXX (also in DD, II, 511–512, 537); Bastide to Ligne, May 25, 1848, DD, II, 449; and Woyna to Lebzeltern-Collenbach, May 21, 1848, AEV. There was a slight delay in the exchange of letters in Paris but for no important reason. See Bastide to Bellocq, June 13, 1848, AEF, Belg., XXX (also in DD, II, 829).

that, because of its principle of neutrality and its geographic position, it would enter into no concert of this nature and reserved to itself its free decision. To show further Belgian goodwill d'Hoffschmidt told Bellocq he would let him in on an important revelation. He had instructed Nothomb to ask d'Arnim two questions: Is the Prussian court disposed to recognize now the French Republic? and, if so, would it first be necessary to coordinate its policy regarding France with other European powers? The answer to the first question was 'yes' and to the second the Prussian cabinet was resolved to act independently of concert with any powers whatever. D'Hoffschmidt specifically asked Bellocq to forward this information to Bastide and in his manner made it clear that he regarded the information as important.[1]

The Belgian concern for formal and close relations with the new republic contrasted with the attitude the French agent in Holland received. Late in May, de Lurde had a friendly talk with Bentinck on the matter of recognition for the Republic. Bentinck claimed that such recognition could not be immediate and singular but rather the natural consequence for Europe after the establishment of a definitive constitution and he went on to mention the problem of status of legislation. He made it clear that the Dutch would follow Britain in granting recognition. Bastide curtly responded to de Lurde that the French Republic did not need to be recognized to exist and to take its place in the world. To sollicit this recognition would not be dignified and France was an integral part of the European family. In fact and right, the Republic was established and that was that. De Lurde was instructed to talk in this vein with Bentinck. It was to be eight weeks before formal Franco-Dutch letters were exchanged.[2]

---

[1] Bellocq to Bastide, May 30, 1848, AEF, Belg., XXX (also in DD, II, 562–563).

[2] Lurde to Bastide, May 30, July 26, 1848, and Bastide to Lurde, June 3, 1848, AEF, Pays Bas, 650 (letters of May 30 and June 3 also in DD, II, 556, 648). In Tallenay's view, the British were hesitating, waiting probably to see the turn of events in Italy. Palmerston pretended it was a matter of form–how was the Queen to write to the Constituent Assembly or to the Executive Commission? See Tallenay to Bastide, June 2 (2 letters), 1848, DD, II, 619–623.

CHAPTER IX

JUNE AND AFTER, 1848

In 1848 the month of brides found Europe still in turmoil from the aftermath of the February Revolution. In a letter to his step-mother on June 7, Prince Albert noted the widespread disorder: Vienna was in chaos and Italy in bloodshed. He was relieved that Belgium and France were still "unshaken" though he observed that "France is on the eve of bankruptcy, and of a Parisian massacre." [1] June was indeed to be the month of massacre in Paris and the success of Cavaignac reassured a host of anxious observers. While Greville found the crushing of the socialists both horrible and savage, to Louis Philippe, Cavaignac's vigor was that of "a brave and good soldier," who was "a downright but honest republican." [2] For Europe, Cavaignac was a relief after a government that, despite words of friendship, had put its efforts into trying to establish other revolutionary regimes. Many in Britain, including Peel, believed that Cavaignac was moving to reestablish some form of monarchy in France, despite the general's reputation for sincerity and known republicanism. To Van de Weyer, Cavaignac's emergence as a strong executive, in effect the successor to the Provisional Government, was a stroke of good fortune for both Belgium and France. [3]

In Brussels the month started in the glow of good feeling on the inauguration of formal official relations. Bastide wrote to Bellocq that he was delighted at how cordial relations were and that a mission that had started under such auspices could only go well. Bellocq especially thanked d'Hoffschmidt for handing along the information that the French would meet with good intentions when they made inquiry at

[1] Martin, *Consort*, II, 70–71. Victoria professed to be more concerned than Albert over affairs in Germany; see Victoria to Leopold, May 16, 1848, LV, II, 205–206.

[2] Greville, *Memoirs*, VI, 86–87, 89. The Prince de Ligne (*Souvenirs*, p. 83) called him a republican of opinion but not of action.

[3] Van de Weyer to Leopold, July 10, 1848, VWP, 116. This was also his opinion in retrospect; see Van de Weyer in Bemel, *Patria*, II, 344. For the Dutch reaction which fit the general pattern, see Lurde to Bastide, July 4, 1848, AEF, Pays Bas, 650.

the cabinet in Berlin.[1] In the friction created by the trial over the murder of a French soldier, Bellocq finally received the court records from d'Hoffschmidt and forwarded them to Paris with word that the military prosecutor in Belgium had put in an appeal against the decision and that now the entire case would be sent before other judges. Regarding Belgian concern over material appearing in the *National*, Bastide indicated that the government in Brussels should not attach more importance to articles in French journals than the French government did to declamations which he maintained could be read every day in certain sheets published in Belgium.[2]

In Belgian domestic politics the biggest news in June centered on results of the June 13 elections. Both the British and Austrian ambassadors reported that the government had emerged greatly strengthened, its reward from the electorate for guiding the state through the trying period since February. In the Chamber the number of spokesmen for ultra-democratic and ultra-republican elements was cut substantially though Castiau was again elected. The Catholic Party's strength was also reduced as the wave of liberal majorities signified extensive popular support. Catholic Party representation became a corps of its wisest and most distinguished statesmen, giving the promise of a responsible conservative opposition. There were no desertions by prominent men from one party to another and the level of political morality in this election was high. Men of integrity led both of the large parties and a sense of mutual respect premeated the political scene in mid-1848. The Liberals basked in their success, enjoying the prestige they shared with the nation for having survived without a vast social revolution. Their Catholic opponents frankly admitted that the election of Liberals in June of the year before had been all that saved Belgium, since the proclamation of a republic in France would otherwise have inspired a similar proclamation in Belgium.[3]

Bellocq was hardly settled in Brussels when he was replaced by Quinette. The urbane and polished Bellocq had enjoyed the confidence of the Belgian government and few people could have replaced him satisfactorily. Quinette, however, was one of these. Bellocq, it was explained to Firmin Rogier, had an insufficient grasp of Belgian

[1] Bastide to Bellocq, June 3, 14, 1848, AEF, Belg., XXX (letter of June 3 also in DD, II, 644). See also *The Economist*, June 3, 1848.

[2] Bellocq to Bastide, June 5, 8, 1848, and Bastide to Bellocq, June 13, 1848, AEF, Belg., XXX (letter of June 8 and 13 also in DD, II, 744, 829).

[3] Walden to Palmerston, June 10, 14, 17, 1848, F.O. 10/138; Woyna to Wessenberg, June 14, 1848, AEV; Discailles, *Rogier*, III, 261–266; Banning in Bemel, *Patria*, II, 493; and *The Economist*, June 17, 1848.

institutions and of the current situation of France. To Firmin's observation that Belgium was well-pleased with Bellocq, Cavaignac merely
said he hoped they would also like Quinette. Of moderate opinions, the
new ambassador had splent his youth in Belgium, as his father had
lived for years at Liège and was well-known and respected there.
Perhaps more to the point, the elder Quinette was a Conventionnel,
as were the sires of Cavaignac and Chazal. Living with his exiled parent,
like Cavaignac and Chazal, he had been educated in Belgium. Thus his
ties with Belgium were especially close and, as Woyna noted, in Chazal
he was assured of the sympathy of a most influential cabinet member.
Quinette arrived in Brussels in early July (7th or 8th) and was at once
introduced to d'Hoffschmidt. After the foreign minister's warm greeting,
he had an audience with Leopold who told him that Belgium would
never forget past French aid. Quinette had an appropriate statement
of friendship which included the remark that neither he (Quinette)
nor the Chief of the Executive Power (Cavaignac) could forget that
their fathers as refugees had found hospitality in Belgium.[1]

On July 24, Quinette wrote a long report to Bastide analyzing Belgian nationality, parties, and institutions. He noted Leopold's stepped-
up social activity since the February Revolution and that the monarch
was now a public symbol of stability and order. France was Belgium's
best customer and good relations with France were considered the best
guarantee for its nationality. In addition, he called attention to a
Belgo-Dutch rapprochement that he could not identify in detail but
noted that only Britain had formerly been so close to Belgium. Quinette
was sure its only object was defense for Belgium in case of a French
attack. However, there were no secret anti-French plots in Brussels
and he believed none would be tolerated by the ministry. Quinette
was convinced that Belgian friendship was genuine and that Leopold
would do nothing to compromise Franco-Belgian relations. In Paris
Cavaignac was affable and conciliatory in conversation with Firmin[2]
and indications augured well for the Belgians while Cavaignac was in
power.[3]

[1] Bellocq to Bastide, July 8, 1848, and Quinette to Bastide, July 9, 10, 1848, AEF, Belg.,
XXX; Walden to Palmerston, June 24, July 11, 1848, F.O. 10/138; Woyna to Wessenberg,
July 12, 1848, AEV; and Firmin Rogier to d'Hoffschmidt, July 5, 6, 1848, CNB, II, 142–145.
[2] Quinette to Bastide, July 24, 1848, AEF, Belg., XXX; and Firmin Rogier to d'Hoffschmidt, July 15, 1848, CNB, II, 152–154.
[3] A slight cloud was to appear when the French began to press the Belgians for payments
covering costs of the French expeditions into Belgium in 1830–31. Cavaignac saw no reason
why such a service should have been free of charge. The Belgian government's reaction was
a stout refusal, supported by Palmerston, coupled with an inference that by such reasoning
Belgium should charge for the expenses incurred because of Risquons-Tout. Earlier Palmer-

From June 26 to July 7, the Belgian parliament met in extraordinary session. Leopold's Speech from the Throne on the 26th mentioned the congratulations which the state had received for its stability and was filled with expressions of praise, pride, and encouragement for the country's successful weathering of a trying period which, for much of Europe, was still going on.[1] Victoria wrote to him that she felt "an uncertainty in everything existing" and that "The prosperity of dear little Belgium is a bright star in the stormy night all round." Part of this "stormy night" for her was the emergence of Cavaignac who might be influenced by his mother, a stern and severe widow of a regicide.[2]

Van de Weyer reported to Leopold that both Victoria and Prince Albert agreed with his outlook on Italian affairs but that the stumbling block was Palmerston who for some time had been in conflict with the court. He reported John Russell as guarding himself from the "impetuosity" of Palmerston. Albert's opinion was that British politicians would do nothing regarding Italy and M. de Tallenay was convinced that the desire to maintain peace was so great at London that the French could invade Italy and chase the Austrians out of Venetia without a war with Britain. Van de Weyer observed that since Cavaignac's coming to power the National was still hostile to Belgium.[3] The mood in Paris was now one of general submission and tranquility while the government was in a period of transition. Little public enthusiasm appeared for the republic which many "despised, detested, and ridiculed." [4]

By August the hotbed of danger was Italy and rumors discussed prospects of a French invasion. Despite pleas from Italy, Cavaignac's disposition was to avoid intervention. Woyna believed this was due to the disordered state of French finances and also the fact that it

ston ventured the opinion that Holland had again become more of a menace to Belgium than France was. See Van de Weyer to Leopold, June 22, 1848; Firmin Rogier to d'Hoffschmidt, July 21, Aug. 4, 1848; Merode to d'Hoffschmidt, July 22, 1848; Van de Weyer to d'Hoffschmidt, Aug. 8, 1848; and d'Hoffschmidt to Firmin Rogier, July 23, Aug. 5, 1848, CNB, II, 118–122, 158–161, 166–168, 187–189, 192–194, 199–200.

[1] HP, II, 701; and Discailles, Rogier, III, 270. For commentary on the changed and much more liberal character of the Belgian Parliament, see The Economist, July 15, 1847.

[2] Victoria to Leopold, July 11, 1848, LV, II, 217–218. Victoria saw things as still stormy three months later (on Oct. 10 to Leopold, ibid., 237–238). Germany's situation was "dreadful," in France "a crisis seems at hand" and Ireland was "quivering in our grasp and ready to throw off her allegiance." For analysis of Belgium's economy after the first six months of 1848, see The Economist, July 29, 1848. Her trade suffered much less than her geographic position might have suggested.

[3] Van de Weyer to Leopold, July 18, 1848, VWP, 116. However, the Belgian government was subsidizing a Parisian paper, in return getting favorable publicity and providing an antidote to such journals as the National. See d'Hoffschmidt to Haussy, Aug. 1, 1848, DM, V.

[4] Greville, Memoirs, VI, 103 (Aug. 20, 1848).

would mean a large enough army to be sure of success. This would
strip garrisons, especially those in Paris, and after the June uprisings
such a weakening was out of the question.[1] A movement was under
way to get Austria to accept Britain and France in the role of mediators
between Austria and Sardinia in Italy. Van de Weyer was in the midst
of these efforts but (contrary to Woyna's estimate) interpreted France
as being strong, with adequate funds and an army of sixty thousand
men poised for invasion. In Great Britain sympathies were divided but
many favored Austria,[2] while across the channel in Belgium popular
sentiment was distinctly anti-Austrian. Within the population the only
significant exception was the former Belgian noblesse who were pro-
Austrian. Leopold himself was particularly interested in the success of
Austrian policy in Italy. Woyna pictured Leopold's views as being far
from those of most of his ministers, Chazal being an exception. The
king's German background influenced him for Austria while in Chazal's
case it was a matter of resenting calumnies heaped indiscriminately on
a brave army. Virtually all Belgian journals praised the insurgents and
condemned Austrian efforts. Both the Catholic party organ, *Journal
de Bruxelles*, and the Liberal ministerial, *l'Indépendance*, consistently
attacked the actions of Radetzky and his army. When Woyna protested, d'Hoffschmidt responded by pointing out problems inherent in
a free press and implied it was beyond his control; his response was,
in fact, the same as the French had just made regarding the *National*.[3]
Rather than the direct refusal expected by Van de Weyer, Austria's
decision on the mediation plan was an insistence on direct negotiations
with Charles Albert. However, if Sardina refused this, then Austria
declared she would accept Anglo-French mediation. Thus Austria
neither accepted not rejected the mediation efforts but found a middle
ground which Cavaignac did not regard as a formal refusal.[4]

The focus of attention for the French was now Italy and Belgium
was secure while Cavaignac was in power. Nevertheless there was still
some concern in Brussels about the prospect of more unemployed
Belgian workers in France wanting to come home.[5] On August 30,
the trial of the prisoners taken in the Risquons-Tout episode ended

---

[1] Woyna to Wessenberg, Aug. 3, 1848, AEV.
[2] Van de Weyer to Leopold, Aug. 15, 1848, VWP, 116. The idea of Anglo-French cooperation as mediators in Italy had been broached earlier on French initiative. Britain's reply
was vague and the Austrians had little regard for British policy in Italy. See Ponsonby to
Palmerston, Apr. 2, 1848, F.O. 7/348.
[3] Woyna to Wessenberg, Aug. 13, 28, 1848, AEV.
[4] Van de Weyer to "Monseigneur" (Leopold), Aug. 31, Sept. 5, 1848, VWP, 116.
[5] See for example, Haussy to d'Hoffschmidt, Aug. 11, 1848, DM, V.

with seventeen death penalties and fifteen acquittals. The severity of
the sentences surprised many observers in Brussels; because, in the
British ambassador's opinion, the evidence against them was not con-
clusive. The British, French, and Austrian ambassadors all reported
little likelihood of actual executions and that all would probably
receive commutations from death to long prison terms.[1] The trial
itself had resulted in an amplification of events shortly after February
24 – particularly of Leopold's offer not to be an obstacle to the adoption
of another form of government if the nation's security required it.
The end of the trial also called attention again to Belgium's example
of stability the six previous, trying months.[2] This stability was celebrated in the third week of September on the occasion of the anniversa-
ry of Belgian independence. The celebrations were especially successful
as the government made a special effort to emphasize both tradition
and progress as well as independence.[3] Leopold basked in all this as
his concerns now became more parochial. Rather than European issues,
he discussed Belgian problems and even his support of Austrian interests in Italy was less emphatic.[4] Austria's problems were to become
more complex but after a fruitless suggestion that Italian affairs be
the subject of special negotiations in Brussels,[5] Belgium was less involved. Indeed, in retrospect Belgian immunity from the full force of
the February Revolution lay in the election of the Liberal ministry in
1847. The Liberals proved in the course of a year in office, as Woyna
observed, to be royalist in Belgian affairs while republican regarding
France.[6] Domestically, with a feeling of security abounding, the
Chamber debates (after November 6) went back to the familiar discussions of saving money in the budget for foreign affairs and complaints that more should be done for Flanders.[7] A semblance of normal-
cy seemed to have returned to Belgian political life.

---

[1] Woyna to Wessenberg, Aug. 31, 1848, AEV; Walden to Palmerston, Aug. 31, 1848, F.O.
10/138; and Quinette to Bastide, Sept. 2, 1848 AEF, Belg., XXX. See Bertrand, *Démocratie*, I,
358–385, for trial and its outcome. Death sentences were commuted. Last of those found
guilty and imprisoned was freed on Feb. 1, 1856.

[2] Woyna to Wessenberg, Aug. 28, 1848, AEV.

[3] Walden to Palmerston, Sept. 26, 1848, F.O. 10/139. For reorganization of Belgian army
and its increased efficiency, see Walden to Palmerston, Oct. 21, 1848, F.O. 10/139. *The
Economist*, Sept. 2, 30, 1848, indicates the sense of calmness and stability in September.

[4] Woyna to Wessenberg, Sept. 20, 1848, AEV. This letter stresses Belgian stability; there
was order without the least effort and the union of the classes behind Belgian institutions
was nearly complete. Leopold was both happy and proud and freely praised the governmental
and administrative mechanism as largely responsible.

[5] Woyna to Schwarzenberg, Dec. 4, 1848, AEV. Bastide favored this idea but successes of
Radetzky altered conditions radically. See Ligne, *Souvenirs*, pp. 77, 81–82.

[6] Woyna to Wessenberg, Aug. 28, 1848, AEV.

[7] HP, II, 720–725, 728.

INDEX OF PERSONS